PRAISE FOR JERRY FORD AND HIS METHOD

"Jerry traveled across the globe to train me. He goes hard in fitness and in life!"

—ALISHA BOE, ACTRESS BEST KNOWN
FOR *13 REASONS WHY* ON NETFLIX

"I am inspired by Jerry's principles of building wealth through real estate and stock market investments as well as entrepreneurship. With multiple streams of income, the sky is the limit when it comes to potential earning power. This book is here to help!"

—ADRIENNE C. MOORE, ACTRESS BEST KNOWN
FOR *ORANGE IS THE NEW BLACK* ON NETFLIX

"Jerry is a beast, and I can totally understand why. Coming from our city, it's life or death."

—DJ MO BEATZ, BEST KNOWN AS BIG SEAN'S OFFICIAL DJ

"Jerry is not only a trainer; he's an entrepreneur. He has come up with incredibly creative ways to service his high-end clientele. Not only do I enjoy working with Jerry—he's great to hang out with."

—MARC WEBB, FILM AND TELEVISION PRODUCER

GUNS, DRUGS, OR WEALTH

GUNS, DRUGS, OR WEALTH

THE THREE-INCOME SECRET TO SUCCESS THAT TOOK ME FROM THE STREETS OF DETROIT TO THE TOP OF MY GAME

JERRY FORD

BEAST PUBLICATIONS

GUNS, DRUGS, OR WEALTH

The Three-Income Secret to Success That Took Me from the Streets of Detroit to the Top of My Game

FIRST EDITION

ISBN   978-1-5445-0094-2 *Paperback*
       978-1-5445-0095-9 *Ebook*

I dedicate this book to anyone who has ever lost a sibling or child. Losing my brother Sam is by far the worst thing that ever happened to my family. It's hard. People don't understand. But hear me when I say, now you can live for two.

CONTENTS

FOREWORD

BY ADRIENNE C. MOORE

When I was growing up, my parents always stressed to me the importance of building wealth and not just riches. They taught me the importance of valuing money, saving it, and—most important—investing it. When I turned eighteen, my mom opened up a savings account for me at a credit union. I can still remember her saying, "Credit unions always give the best interest rates and loans." For my twenty-first birthday, she opened up my first Roth IRA account, because I had started working and she wanted to teach me how to invest my earnings right away. With all of this guidance, you would think I was on my way to building a successful financial life—but I wasn't.

At thirty, I took a major chance on myself and my career

and wound up moving to New York City to earn an MFA in theatre. Before too long, I was a struggling actor with barely any money and thousands of dollars in credit-card debt. I owed well over $100,000 in student loans and could barely meet my basic needs.

What a picture I'd painted for myself. Talk about stressed out—I was getting daily calls from credit collectors! I remember the day I hit rock bottom. I was looking over one of my credit card statements and agonizing over the minimum balance, which was about $120. I began to calculate how many months (years, really) it would take me to pay off the entire amount. When I focused on the card's monthly interest rate, it dawned on me: By paying the minimum, I was doing little more than covering the interest! Only about *one dollar* of each payment was being applied to the principal balance. I was floored, to say the least. How would I ever get out of this pit?

I found myself trying to figure out how a girl who had been taught solid principles of finance and wealth-building had ended up in this situation. I promised myself then and there that I would climb out of that hole and do everything in my power to remain financially free, out of debt, and building wealth for myself and my family. What had happened to me once would never happen again. My early experience with debt taught me a lesson I would never forget: I would never again let my finances get out of my control; I would never spend money that I didn't have; and I would absolutely never EVER pay a minimum balance on a credit card. I would do my best to pay every debt in full every month.

So, how does staying out of debt relate to building wealth? That's where this book comes in. As Jerry Ford details here—and I agree—systemic criminalization of African Americans (mostly men), is the new slavery, and debt plays as big a part in enslaving black America as our judicial system does. No one can build wealth if they are in debt.

I am inspired by Jerry's principles of building wealth through real estate and stock market investments as well as entrepreneurship. With multiple streams of income, the sky is the limit when it comes to potential earning power.

If you're like me, you want to invest more and often try to figure out how to do it—but you find yourself getting sidetracked and losing focus because you just don't know where to start. This book is here to help! In it, Jerry breaks down the principles of sound investing and shows you step by step how to get started.

I once heard someone say that money screams but wealth whispers. I couldn't agree more. When I look at my wealthy counterparts (and I'm talking *wealthy*) you'd hardly know how wealthy they are just by looking at them. Sure, they have nice homes and quality cars, but their money is tied up in the stocks or properties that they own and rent out, or in artwork they purchased as an investment. Their wealth may not be so visible in their everyday lives, but I hear them talk about it. I am inspired by them, and aspire to have that kind of wealth in my own future.

I hope that, like me, you will explore the principles that Jerry illustrates in this book. I hope his ideas and tools inspire you to look beyond the immediate and temporary gratification of buying the kind of expensive things that eventually fade in monetary value. I hope this book inspires you to live a debt-free life while building wealth for yourself and generations to come.

Now GO. BE. GREAT!

Adrienne C. Moore is an American actress best known for her role as "Black Cindy" in the Netflix series, Orange Is the New Black.

PROLOGUE

LIFE OR DEATH

Everything I do is life or death. I keep the stakes high because the pressure that comes with it brings magic out of people. It doesn't matter if I'm working out in the gym, investing, or eating pizza—it's life or death, I go hard. When I step onto the gym floor, I act as if I'm stepping onto the battlefield. My boots are tight, I am geared up, and my "A" game is all I have. My vision is tunneled and I'm not afraid of a blow or a wound, because pain is weakness I expel from my body. I imagine the end of the workout but I don't spend too much time there, because too much thinking about home takes you out of the moment—and that can get you killed. I stay in the moment. I don't think ten steps ahead, I *am* ten steps ahead. I know the difference.

Every step, every move is calculated and has meaning. If it's required, I pivot and improvise as if the new moves were premeditated. I train hard so that fights are easy. I study myself and—more important—I study my opponent.

As Sun Tzu says in *The Art of War,* "If you know the enemy and know yourself, you need not fear the result of a hundred battles. If you know yourself but not the enemy, for every victory gained you will also suffer a defeat. If know neither the enemy nor yourself, you will succumb in every battle."

I analyze my opponent and I analyze myself, because if I don't study both I will lose every time. I go hard but I make it look effortless. I go hard with a smile, I go hard with a grin, I go hard as I laugh, I go hard when I pray, and I go hard with a mean mug. You have to be the best for as long as your best lasts, because you can only stay on top for so long.

Go hard—just don't take yourself too seriously.

INTRODUCTION

First things first: Because people get it twisted but it's all good, I'm going to clear it up. What is wealth? It's not how much you make, it's what you accumulate. Wealth is when you don't have to work to maintain the lifestyle of your choice because you have income from multiple assets. Those assets are investments that you have made.

My name is Jerry Ford and I work as a personal trainer in New York City, Los Angeles, Miami, and London. I am based in LA, but I often travel from coast to coast and country to country to train my clients. Additionally, I am an investor in stocks, real estate, and whatever else makes sense. If it makes money, if the yields are attractive, and if I believe it is worth the risk, I'll invest in it. But before all of these things, as Jay-Z would say, "I'm not a business man, I'm a business, man."

No, seriously, *I am a business.* You are a business—regardless of whether you're a one-man show (trainer, doctor, massage therapist, artist, etc.) or an employee of a company. Every area in which I choose to derive income requires me, the "business," to present myself in an honest, attractive way and conduct business as if my life depends on it. The proof is in the pudding.

How do I conduct business optimally? How do I best present myself? Two words: *diagnose* and *prescribe.* You have to diagnose and then prescribe. You're probably reading (or listening) to this thinking, "Jerry, what are you talking about?" I'm talking about really solving people's problems. I'm talking about really listening to your customers and giving them exactly what they need, rather than offering some general service that is so routine for you that it's easy. Can you imagine going to the doctor, telling him that you have severe migraines, and having him prescribe medication for acne? Your headache won't be cured because the doctor did not listen to you, diagnose your problem, and prescribe an appropriate remedy. It's the same with every business. As a trainer, my job is to listen to what my clients want to achieve with their bodies, examine the challenges they may face, and prescribe a workout and diet plan that will help them reach their goals. *I am my business.*

When someone is contemplating investing in a company,

he starts by scrutinizing the people who represent it. He looks into such things as, "What's the company's reputation?" and "What kind of people work for the company?" The investor is looking for good people who believe in what they are selling or creating, who show up on time, have a positive attitude, can inspire and lead others, and have the boldness to push through. Are you one of those people? Or are you a person who is all talk and no action; someone who doesn't keep his word; someone who can't pivot when necessary and make good split-second decisions? Do you always think you're right? When something goes wrong, do you look in the mirror and blame yourself first, or do you look out the window and blame others?

Your wealth will be defined not just by your investments, but also by others investing in you. Before a smart person invests in a company, he evaluates that company's leader. Be the person who blames himself before blaming others. Be the person who takes extreme ownership.

As this book progresses, I'm going to show you how I took the money that I made as a personal trainer and multiplied it 100 times. I'm also going to explain how I started to build my wealth by developing three forms of income. Most important, I will share the secrets that schools don't share—secrets that will become *your keys to building wealth for yourself.* These secrets will help you live an extraordinary life.

I wrote this book for anyone who wants to build wealth, and that's at least half the world—the more than three billion people who live off two dollars and fifty cents per day. I wrote this book for people in every country who seek the knowledge that can help them break their chain of poverty. I wrote this book for the eighty percent of Americans who work paycheck to paycheck. I wrote this book for my black brothers and sisters in America, but more importantly across the globe. I wrote this book for the people who continue to work hard and put in long hours, but find themselves in a rat race because their employers don't value them for what they are worth. Too many Americans struggle every day. For all of them, I have written this book in simple layman's terms, so that anyone—regardless of educational background or financial experience—can benefit from it. As I wrote it, I imagined myself having a casual front-porch conversation with my readers and listeners. Let's cut to the chase. Let's keep it simple. Let's be real.

Please take note: I'm not *wealthy*, but I am *building wealth*. My financial life is a journey in progress, and I want to share that journey with you. Why? Because the joy is in the doing, *the joy is in the journey*. We fitness folks call it respecting the process. And so far, my process—my journey—has been a success. I'm not here to lecture you; I'm here simply to share my experience and tell you what really works.

The only thing that I ask of you while reading or listening to this book is that you accept the possibility of a new paradigm. I'm asking you to put on a fresh pair of glasses. Go ahead, I'll wait. Don't know what I mean? OK, OK, let me break it down for you so that it can forever be broke. We all have a particular way we see things in life. That's our *paradigm*, our imaginary glasses. It's the way we naturally see people and situations, and it affects the way we respond to people and the way we act in every situation. I'm asking you first to acknowledge that you tend to see things a certain way, and then to change it up. I want you to take off your imaginary glasses. Really. Guys, look: I know this seems silly, but just roll with me on this, OK? Take those old glasses off...and now put a new pair on.

This new pair of glasses symbolizes a fresh vision; a new way of seeing things. Let's try them out. Let's say a friend or family member stole $100 from you. Wearing your old glasses, you probably would have wanted to punch that person in the face (or something equally forceful). Equipped with your new glasses, your new perspective, maybe you'll see another way to handle the situation. Maybe you'll talk to that person and genuinely try to understand why he took the money before deciding on a punishment.

I want you to get used to accepting different paradigms. I want you to get used to looking at common situations from new points of view. In this way, you'll learn more about others—and about yourself. Once you can understand someone's problem, you can help him solve it. And when you can really *diagnose* and then *prescribe,* you will be unstoppable.

So, now that you have your new glasses on, you can be open to new ways of doing things. This is important in understanding my own unique way of creating wealth. The way I am doing it it may be your way, too—or this book may inspire you to find your own way. Seth Godin said it best in his book *Purple Cow*: "If you acknowledge that you'll never catch up by being the same, make a list of ways you can catch up by being different." In sharing my message, I ask you to let me motivate, inspire, and entertain you.

I was born and raised on the east side of the "D"—D-Town—also known as Detroit. I was surrounded by gangs, drugs, guns, crack heads, killings—you name it, I saw it all. I've lived in shelters and I've been homeless. As sad as this sounds, I remember a hilarious story from when my family and I were living in a shelter. One day, while we were out, someone stole a bunch of our possessions. They stole my brother's radio and playing cards—even my Batman drawers. I was devastated. My brother Sam went on a mission to find those Batman drawers, but instead of coming back with the ones that were taken, he came back with grown-man drawers with dark stains on them. You do the math.

Despite how terrible this sounds, it was funny at the time and still makes me laugh today. I love my city because every moment leads to the next and what doesn't kill you makes you stronger. Detroit made me a survivor. It made me who I am today. There is something magical about Detroit, and it's not just that it's the "Motor City" and brought forth some amazing musical talent. There is something about growing up in Detroit, something about the hustle, about surviving, and about making it out. Whenever I say, "I'm from Detroit," I feel powerful. As one of my fellow Detroiters—Big Sean—says, "People say if you can make it in New York you can make it anywhere, but if you can make it out of Detroit, you can make it everywhere."

I wrote this book because I know what it's like to be broke. I know what it's like to feel helpless because you lack the specialized knowledge that might help you reach your goals. They say ignorance is bliss, but really, it just hurts. I wrote this book because I believe that everyone should have an equal opportunity to gain the knowledge he or she needs to build wealth. The problem is, everyone learns differently. This doesn't make one person smarter than the next, but it does require a teacher who takes the time to figure out how best to teach each person. Sadly, a very small percentage of Americans attend the kind of schools—mainly private schools—with these teachers. Only ten percent of Americans can afford private education.

One book can't make up for the deficits in our educational system—I wish it could. But this book is meant to be like having Jay-Z or Warren Buffet coach you personally on how to build wealth by understanding the three forms of income. I want you to have a cool and fun experience reading it, while gaining valuable, specialized knowledge. I want you not just to gain knowledge, but to *become knowledge.*

Most of my teachers laughed and told me that I would never amount to anything because my reading wasn't the best. My mother lost her home because of a lack of understanding of real estate. No one taught her how to reap the benefits of owning a home. No one told her how much money she could have saved in taxes by writing off the costs associated with fixing up our home.

If I had understood the word *responsibility*—which literally means *the ability to choose your responses*—when my brother Sam was killed, I would have made better choices. When my Auntie Sandra was killed, I would have made better choices. When my best friend Steven was killed, I would have made better choices. When I lost others to violent crime and found myself starving from a lack of money, I would have made better choices.

Eighty percent of Americans are middle class, working class, or poor. About ten percent are upper class, leaving less than ten percent as financially free. The average income on the planet is about $1,480 per month, and (as I noted earlier) roughly three billion people live on $2.50 per day. What do we make of these statistics? I believe that the information in your head determines what's in your hand—but it's also true that what's in your hand determines what's in your head. I read or listen to one book a week. The information I've gleaned from them has literally saved my life.

As I stated before, ignorance is not bliss; that shit just hurts. It hurts because it makes you suffer. I have studied many books, learned from them, and personally picked the brains of high-net-worth individuals. I have done this so that I can share the key points with you and take out all the air, all the fluff that doesn't matter. I have tapped into the minds of some of the wealthiest and happiest people in the world and I am going to give you their timeless principles straight up and in layman's terms. My wisdom comes from the people from the suburbs and the people from the ghettos—the Warren Buffets as well as the Jay-Zs.

As I told you, growing up in Detroit, we were broke. Like, broke-broke. Like, moms-freeze-that-chicken-for-six-months broke. Like no heat, no lights, no water in the wintertime broke. And for those of you who don't know,

Detroit can go below zero degrees. It was so cold that me and my brothers, cousins, aunties, and everyone else that lived in my home would sleep in one room with an electric heater. During these times, we did everything in our coats. I mean everything. We slept, cooked, played charades, and got beat by moms, all in our coats. When we had no heat or hot water, we would put a pot of cold water on the electric hot plate until it got really hot, then pour it in the tub so we could bathe. It took maybe four or five pots to fill up that bathtub, which sucked because by the time you heated up the next pot, the water in the tub was freezing again!

How did I handle it? I decided to do what Master Willie, my martial arts master, told me and practice "mind over matter." In other words, I just took a cold-ass shower. As I got older, I realized that Master Willie wasn't actually referring to circumstances like mine, but I applied his words of wisdom anyway. I froze my ass off in that shower, but I must say, I smelled great!

When the lights were cut off, we made best friends with candles. There were literally candles all over the house. It's amazing how beneficial a dollar store can be. Although this sucked just like everything else, our "mood lighting" came in handy when it was time for scary stories. Our scary stories consisted of my older brother Sammy scaring the shit out of me and our oldest brother Bazz scaring the shit out of him. You try being cold and scared. It's no fun, but it's the price you pay for being the youngest.

Now, where was I? Oh yeah, we were broke. My mom took a two-hour bus ride every day to this terrible factory job that paid only five dollars an hour. How she raised three boys on that salary still blows my mind. What can I say? She's a beast. She made it look easy, although I knew then and know now it wasn't.

Understand that I don't tell you all of this to earn your sympathy. As I stated earlier, every moment brings you to the next, and where I came from made me the man that I am today. I tell you these stories to make you understand that you can build wealth regardless of where you come from. If I can do it, you can, too.

The city that made me the man I am today: Detroit.

This book is for you if you are interested in being financially free. If you want to build wealth, this book is for you.

If you have a corporate mindset, it's for you. If you are an artist, it's for you. If you are an investor, it's for you. If you are dirt poor and don't want to be, it's for you. And even if you are a trust-fund baby, it's for you. If you want more time with your loved ones, this book is for you. This book is about money and happiness, and it's about Benjamin Franklin—i.e., the man on all those hundred-dollar bills!

While it's true that money can't buy happiness, it *can* buy you what I like to call *special time*. Special time is the time you devote to the people who matter most to you. Over seventy percent of people in this world spend more than fifty percent of their time working to provide a living for themselves and their families. Can you imagine what it would be like if you could take most, if not all, of that work time and turn it into *special time* with your loved ones?

People love to say that money isn't everything, and they're right. Money is not everything—until it is. Whether you want to admit it or not, money is connected to more than you realize. It's the number-one cause of arguments in America, and the reason behind over fifty percent of all divorces. More than half of businesses fail because of financial problems. People take jobs that they hate for many reasons, but ultimately, it's because they can't afford not to. Sometimes being broke comes from poor decision-making, but that's another story we'll get to later. It doesn't matter who you are, what you've been through, or where you are from. What matters is your drive and willingness to learn specialized knowledge, make a plan, and execute it. Everyone deserves a chance to be free financially. And with financial freedom comes special time with your loved ones.

CHAPTER 1

THE BEGINNINGS

In May of 2010, on the first day that I moved to New York City, I wandered into the New York Health & Racquet Club. NYHRC is a luxury gym with over a dozen locations in the city. On any given day, it is filled with celebrities and high-net-worth members. I went because I wanted to work out, but I wasn't a member, nor did I have the money to join this fine establishment. So, I did what anyone would in this situation: I attempted to get a free trial. I walked in and started sweet-talking the young lady at the front desk. I told her she was beautiful and that I loved her outfit. She looked at me like she'd heard this line a million times. I could see right away that she wasn't really buying it, so I moved on to Plan B. I told her I was new in town and looking to join a gym, but wanted to test the waters before committing to a membership. I was expecting some pushback, but she was actually really nice about it and agreed immediately to let me try the place out. In that moment, I realized that honesty and kindness work much better than manipulation. I could have saved myself a lot of time if I'd tried that in the first place.

In no time, I was hitting the weights. I remember the day like it was yesterday. I did chest and back, followed by some martial arts moves in the mirror—which got me some attention from the lovely ladies in their fancy fitness outfits. Yes. I was *that guy* that day—the one with the eye-catching moves that don't quite belong in a weight room.

Anyway, as I was finishing up, a tall black dude, who I later learned was a trainer at the gym named Claude, turned to me and said, "Yo, playa! What's your name?"

"My name is Jerry—Jerry Ford," I said, as if I were James Bond.

"You're pretty shredded," he told me. "Do you want a job?"

This guy must be kidding me, I thought. *Me? Work at NYHRC one day in New York City?* Then I realized that he hadn't specified what type of work. "Man, I'm not cleaning no toilets!" I told him.

He laughed and said, "No, man, I'm talking about as a trainer."

A trainer. YES. I began to think about all the exciting things that would come with my new job as a personal trainer at a nice gym. *The girls, the free membership...the girls...the free membership...*

When I was done daydreaming, I said, "Yeah, I guess I could fit it into my schedule," trying to suppress my excitement. Beyond my thoughts about the girls and free gym time, I have always had a deep passion for working out that fills me with an enormous amount of joy. I've often said that if I were homeless again but had a free membership to a luxury gym, I would be set. I don't need anything else— just a place to go hard. So, thanks to this tall black dude named Claude, I became an NYHRC personal trainer with all the free gym time I could possibly want.

Claude introduced me to the top trainer there at the time, Rafael, whom I looked up to a lot in my early days of training. As he showed me the ropes, I realized immediately that the real work would be getting clients. How was I going to do that? I learned that I'd either have to poach them straight off the gym floor, or get contact information from the personal training manager and cold-call them to set up appointments. The protocol was to give them a free workout and then try to sell them a training package. In some cases, members would see me training, like what they saw, and approach me for a session. Right from the start, I had a very natural way with people. I was likeable, serious about helping my clients get results, and hungry to do well. I had my eye on that top trainer spot.

As I learned from my amazing fellow trainers at NYHRC, I quickly rose to the top and started training some amazing people. I trained celebrities, Wall Street businessmen and women, and a wide variety of tastemakers. I was killing the game! I'd never known that I could make so much money as a personal trainer while simultaneously getting the best high from changing people's lives through fitness. As time passed, I became really great friends with a lot of my clients. We would go out together, party together, and work out together even when I wasn't training them. Life was great but not as great as it was going to get. Hanging with rich clients had another benefit for me that I didn't see coming. It was the reason that my wealth clock really started ticking.

If you have ever been around extremely wealthy people—I'm talking hundreds of millions and billions of dollars—you understand what I am about to say. Once you get a taste of that lifestyle, all you can think is, *I want this.* You start daydreaming about all the things that you could do and have if you were in their shoes. In that moment, you are willing to do almost anything and learn whatever you need to in order to get to that level of wealth.

Well you can. And this is how it started for me. *You are*

what you are around. When you spend time with people, you start to inhabit their habits. Subconsciously, you start to act like them. Without even trying, you pick up their mannerisms, characteristics, etc. This can be a good thing or a bad thing. Here is where it gets confusing. I told myself that it was a good thing that I was hanging with this crowd of six hedge-fund kids who were just a bit older than I but who made ten times what I did. Sure, they were fun and cool, good clients, good friends, and successful—but there's no way I could keep up with their lifestyle no matter how hard I tried. And I did try. I followed their lead on cars, watches, suits—all that stuff. But, what was play money to them—loose change—was hard-earned for me. It was everything I had.

Don't get me wrong, I was making great money, but I was spending it as fast as it came in. Didn't matter though; I was living life. I leased my first new 5 Series BMW before age twenty-three. When I showed up at the gym, a restaurant, on a first date, people were impressed. You know... that look that people give you when they are amazed at what you have accomplished? That look that lets you know that you have indeed kicked ass? That look that makes you want to keep reaching for the stars? Yeah, it's dangerous but, hey, YOLO, let's keep reaching.

Six months after I leased that beautiful car, I gave it to my girlfriend at the time, Rokeya, and leased the new 650i convertible. This $100,000 BMW was fully loaded with every feature that you can think of, and sat oh-so perfectly on twenty-inch rims. I remember asking David, the guy who leased me all of my cars, to take a million pictures of me next to it to put on the 'gram—Instagram, that is.

When I drove it off the lot I called my brother Lawrence to tell him about my new toy. The first five minutes of that conversation consisted of a lot of loud yelling and celebrating. I was hyped, and I knew that he understood the feeling because he's a successful dentist with a lot of luxury cars of his own. I told him that the first thing I was going to do to this Beamer was get all-black rims and tint the windows. I had it all planned out, all-black everything. He took a deep breath and said, "Jerry that's a $100,000 car. When you spend that kind of money on a car, you don't do anything to it. You especially don't tint the windows, because you want people to see who's in that mothafucka!" Those were his exact words. So I left it as-is and proceeded to be a boss.

There was nothing like driving this car, nothing. I mean, I felt like I was driving a spaceship. Not that I've ever driven a spaceship, but I figured because this car rode so well that a spaceship must feel similar. Anyone who has ever lived in New York City knows that the traffic can drive you crazy—it's bumper-to-bumper for most of the day. I didn't care. All that mattered is that I was in my spaceship, cruising down the streets of the city, playing "Empire State of Mind" by Jay-Z and thinking, *this is what it feels like to be on top.* (Seven years later, on his album *4:44*, Jay-Z would say, "I bought every v12 engine, wish I could take it back to the beginning"—but I had no way of knowing that at the time.)

Now, I understand that I was definitely not on Jay-Z's level, but I was living. Here's the thing: That fancy car came with a lease payment, an insurance payment, and rent on two garages. Total it up and it was almost $3,000 a month—just for the car. But I was living. I was making money, so I would say to myself, "Money ain't a thang."

Six months later, I decided that I needed a brand-new motorcycle to go with the collection. I needed something new. You know, something to keep the fans guessing. Shortly after I bought the motorcycle, I decided to try a 911 Porsche. Sometime after that, I bought the new 2014 Stingray because—naturally—I needed a weekend car. I also needed a couple Rolexes and a couple Ulysses Nardin watches, because watches hold value and are great conversation starters. Watches don't depreciate, right? Right. I also needed that new coat from Bergdorf Goodman and some fresh suits because I have to look the part, right? The list went on and the purchases and the need for more never stopped.

I had convinced myself that this was all OK, even though I

was saving only a fraction of what I made. I had convinced myself that it was all about perception, that my liabilities were actually assets.

I. Was. Wrong. I was doing it all backwards—literally, backwards. I was buying liabilities that I thought were assets.

Let's talk about liabilities vs. assets. *Assets* are things that you own that can provide benefit in the future. Cash, inventory, accounts receivable, land, buildings, and equipment are all assets. Assets are things that put money in your pocket. *Liabilities*, on the other hand, are all of your obligations. They are money that has to be paid or services that have to be done. Credit cards, the lease on a car, the mortgage on a boat or house, loans, all of these are liabilities. Liabilities are things that take money out of your pocket.

Here is the secret about assets and liabilities, and it's something wealthy people all understand. Wealthy people buy only assets and then let the income from those assets pay for their liabilities. Let's dig deeper. The difference between the rich and the poor is that the poor work hard for their money and the rich let their money work hard for them. Poor people buy liabilities that they think are assets and rich people buy assets they know will pay for their liabilities. For example, when a poor person buys a luxury car, the payment comes out of his or her pocket, (i.e., paycheck) every month. The car is a liability because it does not make money, it takes money away. Conversely, when a rich person invests in real estate, that property makes him money, which he can use to buy a luxury car. Do you see? *He's letting the asset pay for the liability.*

JERRY FORD PRINCIPLE 1: BUY ALL ASSETS AND LET YOUR ASSETS PAY FOR YOUR LIABILITIES.

CHAPTER 2

MEETING BILL

I was now one of the top trainers at my gym. I had the best clients and was doing almost 200 sessions a month. I was in the gym from dusk until dawn. I had earned my stripes. I loved my job and I looked forward to coming to work every day. I felt like the badass version of what Amy Cuddy talks about in her book *Presence: Bringing Your Boldest Self to Your Biggest Challenges*: powerful.

I stood tall in this gym. I radiated as if I could blow every single weight down with one breath. No one could tell me anything—I felt like I owned the place. I have never had a nine-to-five job, sat behind a desk, or been a corporate type, but I'm sure that being a hotshot lawyer or a wolf on Wall Street feels similar. I'm sure it makes you feel invincible, just as I did.

I remember my PT manager at the time, Mark Braham (R.I.P.), pulling me into his office to tell me that he had a hot lead for me. That meant a client guaranteed to train at least three times a week for a long period of time, so I was all ears. A hot lead meant money. Mark told me that the client he had in mind had already purchased 200 sessions and that he wanted to train *every day*. At that, my mouth dropped open. *Two hundred sessions?* It was unheard of. The most that gyms tended to sell at one time was 100. *What kind of idiot would come into a gym and drop $20,000 on personal training?*

Needless to say, I told Mark that this client would be in good hands with the one and only Jerry Ford.

This client was going to take me to the next level. He was training every day of the week and all he wanted was abs—at least that's what he told Mark. This was going to be easy money and that meant more cars, watches, and other toys for me. I went home and told all my friends about this new rich guy I'd be training. I made jokes about how he'd better be ready for the ass-kicking I was about to give him. What can I say, I was young and on top.

Boy was I in for a surprise.

The next morning, I woke up at five a.m. to meet the guy, whose name was Bill. He wanted to do his workouts at six in the morning and that was fine with me. I made a point of getting my day started right, with the proper nutrients, so that I'd be fresh and alert for work. I had a protein shake, took my supplements and vitamins, and headed to the gym in my 650i BMW. I had my Rolex on my wrist, diamond studs in my ears, and my brand new white Air Force Ones on my feet. New Adidas pants and a tucked-in-tight Adidas muscle shirt completed the effect. I looked like a trainer, but more important, I looked like money.

If you look like money, people don't have a problem spending money to work with you. I was ready to get that money by getting this man some abs. I arrived at the gym about fifteen minutes early, so I could be at the front desk waiting for Bill. I understood that it was important he knew that I was prepared for him in every way. After all, a client can only be as good as his trainer.

I waited patiently with a smile on my face—a genuine one. At six a.m., an older white guy walked in wearing a suit and tie, his briefcase in one hand and his gym bag in the other. He stopped at the front desk and said his name was Bill, and that he was there to see Jerry Ford.

I politely interrupted. "Bill? I'm Jerry Ford, it's nice to meet you," I said as I extended my hand.

He looked at me strangely, as if he was surprised at what

he saw. He extended his hand and replied, "Yeah, OK. How old are you, kid?"

"I'm twenty-three going on forty," I replied, attempting to reassure him that I was just as good as anyone, young or old. I was trying to gain his respect.

"Yeah, OK. That's what she said. I'm gonna get changed and we'll see what you got." With that, he walked into the changing room.

I was a bit nervous after that. This guy was a fast talker—a real New Yorker. A New Yorker in finance. *This may not be as easy as I thought* went through my head, but I quickly got myself together. *He's gonna see what I got alright.*

He came out and we hit the weights. I thought it was strange that Bill only wanted to do abs, but he had it made up in his mind that the only thing wrong with his body was a weak core. Boy, was he wrong—but I knew that it would be best if I just gave him what he wanted, for the first session anyway. We could ease into the rest later. As I took him through his workout, I discovered something about Bill: He was an asshole. I mean, a true asshole. Bill was the type of asshole who makes you shake in your boots with his wit but also makes you want to punch him in the face.

He would tell me that I was too young to know anything,

and would sometimes dismiss exercises I suggested before even trying them. Before we finished each exercise, he would already be asking me what we were doing next. At one point, he said, "Tell me what we are doing for the entire session. Go!" It was as if he was fucking timing my response! Bill was really pissing me off. I tried my best to give him a good workout but it was impossible because he refused to do half of the exercises.

After his first session, I said to myself, "I have to stretch this fucker." I had a bit of an attitude, but was trying my best to maintain my professionalism. You know those people who live for corporate/business conflict? Who love it and eat it up? Well, that was Bill. Remember, I'm from Detroit! I know conflict, but in my world, you beat someone up, then go about your business. Here, as you can imagine, things were a bit different. I couldn't punch this old white man in the face. *Or could I?* OK, fine, I couldn't, but you catch my drift. So I stretched him, and as I sent him on his way, he looked at me and said, "See you tomorrow morning at six. Be better tomorrow, kid." And then he said something that no trainer ever wants to hear. He said that the workout could have been harder. When he said that, I'm pretty sure my inner self jumped over the table and choked him all the way to the end. In real life, I just looked at him, smiled, and said, "OK, Bill. See you tomorrow."

The other trainers told me that they would not have tolerated the guy. They kept saying how they would have sent him home as soon as he started acting out. I was pissed and embarrassed, and felt pushed into a corner. My ego was a bit hurt and I had no idea what to do. Training Bill was going to be torture and I knew it, but I didn't know what to do about it.

Sure enough, the next day was worse than the first, and the day after that was even worse. Bill's behavior got so bad that I would play out full scenarios in my head on my way to work at five a.m., all the things I wanted to do to my client. I guess we all do this sometimes, when we have a strong feeling about someone. We play out both positive and negative responses, anticipating what we might say and do.

In this case it was tough to come up with any positive scenarios. It got to the point where I would be driving along, saying to myself, "If he pulls his usual shit today, I'm going to say, 'Fuck you, this is my gym, GET OUT, YOU BITCH!'" I imagined myself beating Bill up and telling him why I was doing it as I was doing it.

For six long months, I dealt with this guy's bullshit every single day of the week. As a kid, I had been to jail, been in gang fights, gun fights, and martial-arts fights, but this was the longest and hardest fight I ever fought and I was determined not to give up. I said to myself, "Jerry, you are from Detroit and there is no way that this old white man is going to scare you." So I kept showing up. Every day, I came with my game face on, ready to go to battle. Detroit. Stand. Up.

On one particular day, I woke up and started my morning as usual. As Bill and I were working out, he was behaving typically, slinging smart remarks and putting me on a timer as he demanded to know exactly what we were doing. As we were working on an incline chest press, he decided to try and convince me that chest presses do not work out the chest muscles. *He actually tried to convince his experienced trainer that lying down on his back, pushing an object up at an incline did not work his chest.*

I couldn't believe the nerve of this guy, who'd never had a muscle on his body before meeting me. I wanted to yell in this dude's face, "You are not a trainer and this gym is not the stock market!" Instead, I popped him on his shoulder and firmly explained how this particular movement works the upper part of the chest. I topped it off with, "This is not finance bro, this is the gym. And when you're in the gym, don't think, just do what I say." I wasn't angry, but I was confident and strong. I was not taking any more shit from Bill, and he must have realized it. He looked at me, nodded his head *yes,* and kept saying to himself, "Kid's fucking twenty-three, what are you gonna do?" It was as if he had been testing me and now he was done. I had finally passed with flying colors.

It felt good to finally shut him up and assume the role of his professional equal. It marked a turning point in our relationship. Bill finally started to respect me and I him. In that moment, I think we both realized we had a lot in common, and that we could truly learn from each other.

Looking back, I think Bill had been testing me because he genuinely had a hard time believing that a twenty-three-year-old could be as good a trainer as I was. And for my part, I didn't want to admit that Bill was by far the smartest, wealthiest guy with the most wit I had ever met. When we were both finally able to openly admire each other, the magic started to happen. We shared our thoughts and opinions, and that led us to form a real connection. We began to understand each other and started to help each other in countless ways.

Once we were able to break down the walls between us, Bill got real results: He was in the best shape of his life. Over time, we not only became good friends in the gym, our friendship unfolded outside the gym as well. I met Bill's wife, his kids, and his friends, and we truly became family. They came to every personal event that I had, and he was there for me in every way possible, advising me on matters of money, women (his personal favorite), you name it. Bill became my mentor. For every holiday, especially Christmas (even though he is Jewish), he would gift me a five-pound tub of "Super Pro" protein and a generous sum of money packaged in a unique way. One year, he framed 100 hundred-dollar bills and I still have them, frame and all. Check out the picture below.

Bill, the client who started me down the path to success, put $10,000 (cash!) into a picture frame and gave it to me for Christmas. I will never spend it.

Triple B and me.

Every day with Bill was a workout for both of us, but I was spending time with my mentor and friend. Training him, telling him what to do, counting reps, and having a full conversation at the same time became easy, despite the hell he'd put me through those first six months.

My relationship with Bill went on for years and I got smarter and wiser by the day being around the man. He helped me save and invest my money in smart ways, and taught me how to take my financial life to the next level. The truth is this: I changed his life and he changed mine.

> ## JERRY FORD PRINCIPLE 2: IT'S NOT HOW MUCH MONEY YOU MAKE, IT'S HOW MUCH YOU KEEP THAT MATTERS.

CHAPTER 3

THE MOVE TO LA

When I was twenty-six, I woke up one day and decided to move to LA. I don't know why, but I knew that I wanted to experience living on the west coast at some point in my life. I also knew that it was better to move while I was still young. It made sense to take bigger risks at a young age. I realized that I would be leaving amazing clients, friends, Bill, and a great business that I had worked so hard to build. But I have always been a risk-taker, so I left. After giving everyone two months' notice, I moved to Los Angeles with no job and no connections.

I shipped all of my beautiful cars and my motorcycle out with me because, hey, it was LA; I knew it was all about what you drive. More than anything, I knew that I was going out there to take over. I had one, maybe two friends there, and crashed at my friend Carlton's place for two weeks. By the end of Week One, I had landed a job as a personal trainer at Equinox. My great friend and client Adrienne (who was kind enough to write the foreword to this book) took me to all of the 2014 Emmy events. I hit the ground running and LA welcomed me with open arms.

I quickly became one of the top trainers at Equinox and started to do some damage. Within six months I had the best clients, including celebrities, more high-net-worth people, and even members of the royal family of Saudi Arabia. Once again, I was the Man. I worked hard and played hard. I worked long hours and spent a lot of money. But this time was different. This time I had the investments that Bill had helped me make and manage, and they were providing plenty of income. I had money invested, *and* I was making money. I was a rock star in LA. I had the nice cars, motorcycle, jewelry, and, thanks to Maeve Reilly, one of my new clients and friends (who also happens to be the best stylist in LA), a new wardrobe.

Once again, I was unstoppable and I was living the life— but it began to bother me that I was still working long hours for another person's company. Not only that: The company was ripping me off, as all gyms do with their trainers. This was not financial freedom. After all, as Robert T. Kiyosaki says in *Rich Dad, Poor Dad,* "A job is a short-term solution to a long-term problem." Sure, I had a job and I was making a lot of money, but this was not the answer. It was time to make some changes in order to really be free financially. I wanted to be wealthy.

I love what I do, but I knew there was no way I could keep training sixteen people a day for the rest of my life. I couldn't scale that even if I wanted to. I can't stress enough how much I enjoy changing people's lives through fitness. When I put in sixteen-hour days, sometimes it doesn't even feel long because I love the people and the art of personal training. It's almost as if I'm on an active vacation. As long as there's good music playing, I'm in the zone and that puts my clients in the zone. I feel as if I could go on forever, but the fact of the matter is, I can't.

My goal was to figure out a way to become a billionaire—or at least get on the right track toward it. There was only one problem: I had no idea where to start. My mind was mainly occupied with selling personal training sessions for Equinox, to make sure they hit their monthly goals. I put everything into holding onto my status as their super-star trainer. Meanwhile, I was training so many people each day that there was no time to think about new strategies.

I prayed about this. I thought about it whenever I could. And—sure enough—shortly after I began praying and thinking about my future, I was fired from Equinox.

Equinox fired me for working out with one of my clients,

even though they had given me permission to do so multiple times. After firing me, they quickly realized that ninety-nine percent of my clients had left Equinox to follow me to a private training gym. Their response was to ban me from Equinox worldwide. To this day, anytime I walk into one of their gyms, somebody kicks me right out. Maybe you think this makes me mad, but the truth is, I totally understand. If I were in their position, and somebody posed a threat to my business, I'd probably do the same thing.

As upset as I was when they fired me, I now feel that Equinox did me a huge favor. This was God answering my prayers. This was what I needed to shake me out of my comfortable routine. By firing me, they forced me to really get on the billionaire track instead of just straddling the fence. I truly believe that the illusion of security stifles ambition. I believe that when we feel too safe and secure, we end up settling for what we have instead of striving for what we want.

I had been spending ten-to-sixteen hours a day, seven days a week at Equinox. I'd even gotten the no-working-seven-days-in-a-row rule waived because the PT manager was happy to rack up the numbers. Although I had income coming in from investments, I was still tied to the gym as long as I knew that there would always be a new client or lead from the PT manager. I was playing it safe. But when I left Equinox, I was motivated to push above and beyond what I'd been capable of.

As I stated before, what doesn't kill you makes you a survivor, and you have to decide to get stronger. I left Equinox and soared as an independent trainer, making four times as much per client as I had at Equinox. Not only that, I was my own boss and loving it.

Now that I had quadrupled my income from training and still had income from my investments coming in, I knew that this was a sign to really take financial freedom to the next level. Here we go. I reinvested all of my profits from my investments because I knew that would put me on the billionaire track. Investing some or all of your profits is the fastest way to attain wealth and compound your money.

JERRY FORD PRINCIPLE 3: THE ILLUSION OF SECURITY STIFLES AMBITION.

CHAPTER 4

THE BILLIONAIRE TRACK

Bill and I talked at least four times a week, sometimes about girls, sometimes about business, sometimes about his family. You have to surround yourself with those that you aspire to be like. One day, I called him to talk about business, real business—I'm talking "billionaire-track" business.

When Bill picked up the phone, I cut straight the chase. "Hey, Triple B [my nickname for Bill], how did you get where you are? Anybody can make one million, but only a small percentage of people make as much as you do."

He was silent for a few seconds, surprised by the depth of the question. To lighten the mood, he joked, "You gotta be good looking and the rest is luck."

I wasn't in the mood for jokes and I didn't laugh. "Triple B," I said, "I'm ready to take this shit to the next level and I need your help."

Again, silence on the phone for a few seconds. Then he asked me when I would be in New York City next, and I told him that I would get on the next plane. I freed up my schedule and headed out of LAX on a red-eye, planning to spend the next twenty-four hours talking to Bill about my plan of attack.

When I landed in New York the next morning, I headed straight to Bill's house, or should I say, his estate. He greeted me at the door and I said, "Let's get to work," but he laughed and told me to slow down and cool my jets. "Get settled," he said. "Get some food and relax."

Now, anyone who knows me, knows that I am the most impatient person in the world when it comes to certain things. I'm 100 percent patient with my clients, but when it comes to going after what I want, I'm impatient. I looked at Bill and said, "OK, fine. But after we eat, we got dead presidents to make."

Looking back on it, he must have thought I was crazy hopping on a plane across the country just to have a conversation. He probably thought we could have talked on the phone—but I knew we needed to plot face-to-face.

As we were sitting and having a meal, Bill said, "What's the difference between an asset and a liability?"

"Dude, are you kidding me? This is no time for your tests and games."

Again, he asked me, "What's the difference between an asset and a liability?"

OK, Bill. We'll do it your way. I explained what he'd taught me: that assets put money in your pocket and liabilities do the opposite.

"Right," he said. "Now, what's the difference between the broke and the rich?"

At this point, I was getting a little annoyed because I didn't know where the hell he was going. "The broke work for cash and the rich make that cash work for them," I said, shaking my head.

He nodded. Then he pulled out a pad and a pen and told me to write all of my liabilities in one column down the page and my assets in another column next to it.

Here's what I wrote:

LIABILITIES	ASSETS
Rent	Stock portfolio
650 BMW payment	Personal Training
Stingray payment	
Porsche payment	
Motorcycle payment	
Insurance for all cars	
Amex credit card payment	
Capital One credit card payment	
Phone bill	
Utility bill	
Clubbing on weekends	
Clothes/Shoes	
Watches	
Luxury restaurants regularly	
ETC.	

It was easy to see that I had many more liabilities than assets.

Now, there's this thing Bill does with his face after he says something really genius or cool. It's kind of like he's shaking his head, squinting his eyes, and tucking his lips inward as he stares at you waiting for you to catch up to what he just said. For the record, I hate it. But he said something that day, made that face, and was right—as usual. He told me to reduce my liabilities and once I'd done it we could talk. We finished our meal, hung out, and I went back to LA.

I guess you could say that I am an all-or-nothing type, somebody who takes things to the extreme. When I got back home, my first priority was to do exactly what Bill had said, so I got rid of all of my liabilities. Not some, but all of them. I sold all of my cars and canceled the insurance payments that went with them. I ditched my motorcycle, paid off my credit cards, stopped buying watches and clothes, and put myself on a budget. None of this was easy, but I knew that I had to make these sacrifices in order to reach my goal. My new budget allotted me just $70 a week for food and I UberPooled everywhere.

My clients and friends thought that I was insane, especially because of the UberPool thing, but I didn't care. I had my mind fixed on being liability-free and building my asset column. By ride-sharing, I was spending only $300 a month for transportation, which was better than leasing or renting the cheapest car in America if you factored in the down payment, gas, car note, insurance, maintenance, and occasional parking tickets.

On weekends, when my friends wanted to go out, I went only if it was within walking distance or fit into my Uber-Pool budget. I was really exercising the "power of broke." Daymond John would be proud.

Once I could show that I had reduced my liabilities, it was time to go back to New York. But, due to the budget I set for myself, I couldn't afford the trip. This time, I used the phone to talk to Bill. I explained how I had gotten rid of everything including my cars.

He was shocked. "I didn't tell you to go carless in LA, Jerry! How are you getting around?"

I laughed and explained the benefits of UberPool. "I guess you can see how serious I am about building wealth," I told him. He may have thought I was crazy, but he couldn't deny my determination. Now that I had prioritized my assets over my liabilities and saved a ton of cash, I was ready to make whatever investment necessary to be financially free.

"Ok Triple B, what's the next step, bro?" I asked, pen in hand, ready to take notes.

The first thing he explained was the benefit of having different forms of income. Any person of wealth has three or more streams of income coming in. This type of income is called *passive* income. Passive income comes from any investments that you have made where all you do is collect. As I have said, wealth is not how much you make, it's what you accumulate.

I'll now tell you to do what Bill advised me to do: Add up all of your monthly costs, including what you spend on luxury items, and multiply that amount by ten. This is the amount of passive income you should aim to have coming in every month. Then, add up your monthly costs and multiply that number by 100. This is the minimum amount of money that you should have saved or invested at any time.

The next thing that Bill impressed upon me was the importance of reading. He gave me a long list of books and told me to read one every week, take notes, and that we would have a conversation each Sunday about what I was reading and how to apply it to my life.

I was silent, thinking to myself, *I don't remember the last time I read a book.* It's not that I can't read, but when I do read, my mind tends to wander less than a page into the book. I had tried locking myself in a silent room. I had tried playing music in the background. I had even tried being a part of a book club and reading with others. None of those things seemed to help—so I was not excited at the prospect of reading, let alone a book a week. I finally spoke up. "Bro, I can't read a book a week, I'm not that smart."

"Jerry, I hate reading, too—so you should do what I do. Try audio books. Listening can be a great way to learn."

This was music to my ears—literally. I realized that all my life I'd had no trouble remembering what teachers said in class—and could apply what I learned that way—but I'd always done badly on tests when I had to learn by reading books. I was twenty-six and had never read a book from cover to cover in my life! Turns out I was a listener and not a reader, but I'd never figured that out until Bill brought it up, and my teachers hadn't either.

I advise you to come to terms with whether you're a reader or a listener, and act accordingly. It's important to know your strengths and weaknesses, because you can only take over the world at your strongest.

All that was left to do was download an audiobook app and all of the books on Bill's list and begin listening. As I worked my way through these books, I realized how much information was out there and how much I had been missing out on. I had been letting the fact that I had trouble reading get in the way of attaining knowledge—and knowledge is the key to success.

It turns out that most CEOs—as busy as they are—manage to read a book a week. If they could do it, so could I. As I listened, I took detailed notes, studied the information, and applied it to my everyday life. When you read something but you don't take notes or remember it, it's as good as not reading it at all. If you read something and take notes but don't apply it to your everyday life, that's also as good as not reading it at all. Stephen Covey, the author of *The 7 Habits of Highly Effective People,* put it this way:

"To learn and not to do is really not to learn. To know and not to do is really not to know."

Working through all those books wasn't easy, but nothing worthwhile ever is. It was simply a matter of building a new habit, which takes an average of sixty-six days to do. Once something becomes a habit, you can then do it effortlessly. You have to bring just enough discipline to bear on the task to get you through those sixty-six days, and you're set. Don't strive to be a disciplined person, strive to have great habits. If your habits are in line with your goals, you will get wherever you want to go. I successfully cultivated the new habit of listening, taking notes, and applying the information to my life. My goal wasn't to *attain* knowledge but to *become* knowledge.

Because I was training ten to sixteen people every day, the only way I could reach my goal of listening to audio books for three hours a day was to do some careful time-blocking. *Time-blocking* is the practice of setting aside explicit blocks of time for specific tasks and making those tasks the priority for that time period. I strongly recommend the practice. During each time block, it's best to turn off your phones and other devices; supply yourself with water and snacks; and cut yourself off from the outside world to avoid the possibility of interruptions. All of this gives your brain a chance to function at the max and your smart and creative ideas to flow effortlessly. Most importantly, time-blocking gives you time to work on your goal. *Give your task time and you will give it life.* As Gary Keller, the author of *The One Thing,* says, "Time on a task, over time, eventually beats talent every time."

My own plan was to schedule one-hour slots throughout the day to listen to books. My first training session is usually at 5:00 a.m., so I started getting up at 3:50 and listening for one hour before work. My next listening slot was during lunch at noon, when I listened for another hour as I ate. My next slot was at 8:00 p.m., after dinner. I'm not going to lie; at first my brain hurt from all the new information going in. But, just as I train my physical muscles, I had to do the same for my brain. And just like my physical muscles, the more I worked my brain by listening and reading, the stronger it became.

Weeks went by as I read, studied, talked to Bill about what I was reading, and applied as many of the timeless principles I was learning as I could. The process actually became fun once I accepted the fact that there would always be more to learn, and that no one knows everything. In fact, the more I learned from the books Bill recommended, the more I realized what I didn't know. I also realized that the moment a person stops searching for knowledge, ignorance begins to take its toll.

Just as Bill had predicted, once I'd developed three forms

of income—which you'll hear about it detail in subsequent chapters—I really began to build my wealth. (Of course, there's no need to stop at three; the more income streams the better. But the basic three will put you on a path to wealth immediately, no matter what order you establish them in.) You can focus on one at a time or all three at once. But I want to stress that it is important to *diversify* your investments. Diversification is beyond important because putting all of your eggs in one basket is way too risky. Diversify, diversify, diversify. Take your time, do your homework, and don't wait—execute as soon as you're ready.

> **JERRY FORD PRINCIPLE 4: DON'T STRIVE TO BE A DISCIPLINED PERSON, STRIVE TO HAVE GREAT HABITS.**

Now, let's get started talking about our first form of income.

CHAPTER 5

INCOME FORM NO. 1 – PASSIVE INCOME FROM REAL ESTATE INVESTING

I called my brother Shabazz, a.k.a. "Fatt Father," and told him that we were going to start a real estate company. Without any pushback, he said, "Let's do it." After going back and forth about a name, we decided to call our company Early Ventures. I am currently the Chief Executive Officer (CEO) and Shabazz is the Chief Operating Officer (COO). Additionally, we have a team of people we work with who specialize in a variety of aspects of real estate.

After deciding on the name, we created a separate entity that would own all of the properties we would buy. We chose to create a limited liability company (LLC) so that our properties would be protected. Creating and using an LLC limits the extent of any liability to only the assets that the LLC itself owns, so that there is no risk to any of your other personal assets. In other words, if something related to your LLC goes south, nobody will come after your house or personal bank accounts.

Once we formed the entity, we started buying real estate—four properties in one year. We had no choice but to pay cash for our first four properties, because banks don't lend to LLCs. The intent of Early Ventures has always been to buy property either to flip it (meaning resell it quickly) or to rent it out. Our mission is to provide people with a beautiful and comfortable place to call home.

Maybe you're thinking you couldn't do what we did because you don't have the cash to lay out. But here's the best part: You don't need money to do this. If you don't have your own money to invest, you can invest other people's. Of course, it's most advantageous to use your own money, but all avenues are good when every road leads to wealth. To show you how it's done, I am going to approach real estate deals from all angles—with money and without money. All you have to do is follow the ten steps I've laid out below, and the advice that goes with them, and you will be on your way to creating passive income.

Note: I am not a lawyer or an accountant, so, before you

embark on a real estate strategy of your own, review your plans with qualified professionals.

STEP 1. UNDERSTAND HOW YOUR REAL ESTATE INVESTMENT PRODUCES PASSIVE INCOME.

Before you can begin investing in real estate, you have to understand all the possible ways you can use it to create wealth. Whether you are buying a home for you and your family to live in or 100 properties to flip or rent out, these are the main ways you can make money from your investments.

- **Loan Pay-down** – If you pay cash for a property, this does not apply to you. If you have a mortgage, it does. Every month, when you make a mortgage payment on a property, you are decreasing the amount that you owe on the overall loan. Remember, you can anticipate getting the money you invest back when you sell the property—but along the way, you can probably write off the mortgage interest and save that way as well. Want to cut your total mortgage payments in half? If you pay the principle mortgage balance a month in advance, you will be paying your mortgage off in fifteen years instead of thirty. (If you can't do the math, there are mortgage calculators on line to help illustrate this point.) If you prepay next month's principle now, and keep that up as long as you own the property, you'll pay it off in half the time. (Don't believe me? Talk to your accountant. This is a trick that all wealthy people know.)

- **Cash Flow** – When you buy an investment property and rent it out, every month you receive cash from your tenants. This is that passive income I keep talking about: cash you're making in your sleep. Money that you are not working for. Although I know how tempting it is to spend this money as it rolls in, here's a word to the wise: Reinvest those profits and you'll get to your goal ten times faster.

- **Saving on Taxes** – To make sure that you are getting all of the tax benefits of real estate ownership, it's best to HIRE AN ACCOUNTANT. Meanwhile, here are some facts you may not know: If you live in your home for at least two years, you can save up to $250,000 as a single person and up to $500,000 as a married couple in taxes when you sell. Please, please, please do not miss out on this. Also, if you live in your home for one year and one day and then move at least fifty miles away, you can also save up to $250,000 as a single person and $500,000 as a married couple in taxes. In addition, if you buy a property—either to live in or as an investment—and you wait one year and one day to sell it, you pay significantly less tax when you sell. They call this "reaping the benefits of capital gains." So when you purchase a property, unless there is a very compelling reason to get out quickly, wait at least a year and one day, people. And when you do sell, ask your accountant about a 1031 exchange. This essentially allows you to trade properties so that you don't have to pay taxes when you sell. For example, if I sell one of my properties to buy a similar one, I don't have to pay taxes on that exchange as I would if I were simply cashing out.

- **Property Appreciation** - In most cases, your property is constantly appreciating. If you buy a property for $100,000 and it appreciates $10,000 in one year, you have made $10,000 without doing anything. In a rare case where it depreciates, no problem, don't panic. The housing market fluctuates but it eventually goes back up. Instead of selling in a down market, just hold on to the property and rent it out until the market gets better. Unless you desperately need a big chunk of money right away, do not let anyone—including your realtor—convince you to sell your home for less than what you paid for it, or less than you believe it's worth. Your realtor may also be your friend, but first and foremost he or she is working to make money—and that only comes from commissions on a sale. Your realtor is in business just like you, and doesn't always have your best interests at heart. Before you sign a contract of sale, make sure you are comfortable with the terms and don't be manipulated. Don't be at the mercy of the market. Trust me. You will thank me for this advice.

STEP 2. BUILD THE RIGHT TEAM.

The right team is essential to anything you're trying to do, but especially to real estate investing. Warren Buffett says, "Price is what you pay, value is what you get," so don't be cheap when it comes to your team. That will cost you in the long run. The following is a list of the team members that I recommend having:

- Someone who has your back and supports you: a wife/husband, partner, brother/sister, friend, etc.
- A good real estate agent: Use a referral, find one in the Sunday paper, or search online for "best realtors in my area." When you call, ask for the manager of the company and tell him or her that you want the best realtor, someone with a lot of experience who has investment property himself. Meet that person and make sure he or she is someone you feel good about spending considerable time with. Make sure the company has a website (most do).
- A skilled lawyer: Lawyers are expensive but necessary in times of need. Search online for local firms and ask the firm to propose someone who works with real estate investors, buyers, and sellers. Some firms require their lawyers to do a certain amount of pro bono (free) work. Call local firms in the area to see if they would be willing to help you pro bono. There are also a few good online legal sites that have great templates if you need to put together very simple doc-

uments such as routine leases. Don't panic if you don't have a lawyer. I didn't have one for a full year after I bought my first four properties. You can't always control what happens on your property, but if you do your homework and screen your tenants properly, it will decrease your chances of needing a lawyer.

- An insurance agent: Always insure all your properties. Call every insurance company that pops up on Google and get rates and details. Compare and choose as you see fit.

- A property manager: You want a management company to manage your property so that you can spend time investing and doing other business, rather than acting as a landlord. The landlord's job is no fun and a waste of an investor's time. If you are spending time replacing lightbulbs, you have lost sight of the big picture!

- An accountant/CPA: Your accountant should have experience working with real estate investors. Be sure that he or she is a Certified Public Accountant.

- A lender: This can be a bank, credit union, or a private/ hard money lender.

- A mentor: Find someone who has been-there-done-that and cares about you, someone who is available to answer your questions, give you a pep talk when you need one, and tell you the honest *truth*. Education doesn't stop when we graduate school—it's just that we have to find our own teachers.

- A bookkeeper: If you are a very organized person who loves numbers, you might be able to keep track of your own books—but I suggest you hire someone to do this and save your valuable time for money-making matters. There are plenty of freelance bookkeepers out there who work by the hour, and there are established firms that work by contract. Check out the ones in your area.
- Trustworthy contractors, including plumbers, electricians, etc.: The best way to find these is to ask friends or go into your hardware or plumbing/electrical supply store and ask for referrals. Sometimes they even have boards where contractors post ads. You can also search online or sign up for referral services such as Angie's List or Home Advisor.

STEP 3. SPOT A DEAL.

- Run the numbers. The first thing to do before you make an offer on a property is do the math. You can't be certain about how much any repairs or other maintenance necessities will cost before having an inspection, which we will talk about later; but this will give you a good idea of whether the property is worth investing in, or if you should walk away.
- Be OK with walking away. Never get emotionally attached to an investment—keep it business all the way. The minute your emotions kick in, the word "investor"

walks out the door. Someone (I wish I knew who it was, so I could credit him or her) said, "Never think with your emotions, use your emotions to think."

- Buy the best. We are investors, at this moment real estate investors, which means that we only enter into good deals. We only buy properties with attractive yields—i.e., the amount of your money that you make back annually from the total amount you spent on the property. How do you calculate the yield? It's the purchase price divided by your annual income (from rent), after all expenses are paid. What expenses? Insurance, taxes, management fees, utilities, etc.

- Be able to distinguish a good deal from a bad one. Some real estate investors consider a good yield to be at least three percent; others feel it should be no less than six percent. Personally, I do deals only when there is a yield of at least ten percent after expenses. I only buy *great* deals. Plug your numbers into the table below to see if your deal makes sense. If it doesn't, walk away.

There are five basic ways to buy real estate, and they each have their advantages and disadvantages.

ADDRESS	PURCHASE PRICE	BROKER/ CLOSING FEE	MORTGAGE	UTILITIES	TAX/HOA	MNGT.	INSURANCE	RENT	NET TO YOU	YIELD
1234 N. Detroit St.	$200,000	$TBD	$0	$1,200	$1,920	(8% FEE) $2,304	$1,200	$28,800	$22,176	11%

1. Cash: The good thing about paying cash is that it's much easier to get a great deal; everyone loves a cash buyer. Paying cash also decreases your monthly overhead, because you have no mortgage payments to make. That means you'll never be desperate to keep the property occupied, so you won't be tempted to rent to unqualified or undesirable tenants.

I'm going to wander off the subject of financing for a minute to talk about this, because it's important. Renting to bad tenants is the last thing you want to do, because evictions are expensive and time consuming. Believe it or not, if you find yourself in a situation where you have to get a tenant out, you might end up being better off *paying him to leave.* Avoid this whole scenario by screening your tenants carefully. Personally, I like to make sure that all of my tenants can show that they made at least three times their monthly rent for the previous four pay periods and that they have no evictions on their record. I also require them to go through a criminal background check.

2. Seller financing: Seller financing is exactly what it sounds like; you are getting a personal loan from the seller to buy the property. The seller acts as the bank and you and the seller negotiate the terms of the financing, including the amount of the down payment, the interest rate, and any penalties for missed or late payments. In most cases, if you were to stop making payments, the seller would operate exactly as a bank would: He would keep all that you have already

paid—including the down payment—and foreclose on the property (i.e., take it back). The moral of the story is, *Don't miss a payment.*

Maybe you're thinking that a seller would be crazy to agree to seller financing, but it's actually quite a common practice, and can be win-win. Here's an example of how it works. A guy is selling his current home for $100,000 and plans to purchase a better one for $200,000. He and the guy who is buying his first place agree on a twenty-percent down payment, which is usually what banks require when purchasing an investment property. That money is enough for the ten-percent down payment on the new place, and the buyer's monthly payments provide the seller with cash every month until the loan is paid off. Seller financing can also save the seller the big tax bill he'd have to pay if he got all the money for his home at once. My strategy would be to take the buyer's down payment, use it as a down payment on my new home, and be sure to negotiate terms and interest rates favorable enough that the monthly payment covered my new mortgage (or most of it). Get creative. Although it helps to have these things, you do not need a bank or a good credit score to buy property. Don't feel bad for pursuing this alternative, whatever the reason.

3. Mortgage: When your plan is to buy property by

taking out a mortgage, it's a very good idea to get pre-approved by a bank before you even start looking for properties. What I'm referring to is a letter from the bank informing all potential sellers that you qualify to borrow money. Pre-approval letters are quite standard, and involve providing the bank with things like pay stubs, bank statements, tax returns, etc. They can take a few weeks to come through (especially if you are disorganized with your paperwork, as I sometimes am), but it's worth the wait. You do not want the frustration of finding the property of your dreams, only to see it sold to someone else while you are in the process of getting bank approval.

Here's something you need to understand, though. A pre-approval letter does not mean that the bank is guaranteeing it will give you a mortgage—just that it *might,* pending further digging into your financial status. For that reason, you have to get a *loan contingency* into your Purchase Agreement. That's a clause in the contract stating that if your bank ends up denying your loan, you can have your Earnest Money Deposit (EMD) back. This is important, as a deposit can amount to thousands of your hard-earned dollars. Don't worry we will discuss banks and loans more later. Stay with me.

4. OPM: One of my favorite ways to buy properties is

OPM, which stands for Other Peoples' Money. If you are serious and really do your homework to find great deals, people will invest in the great projects you find. You can negotiate their share of the ultimate profits as you see fit. For example, if Katie doesn't have money for a down payment, but has a great credit score and a consistent job and income, she can partner with Nate, who has cash but bad credit, on a deal. The partnership is good for both because each brings something unique to the table: One of them supplies the cash and the other is able to get the mortgage. In a deal like this, I typically structure it so that eighty percent of all profits go to the person who fronted the cash (here, that would be Nate) and twenty percent of all profits—plus the tax break—go to the person who obtained the mortgage (in this case, Katie).

You can also come to an agreement about when you want to discuss selling the property—depending on the market, of course. If you agree to wait at least a year and one day before considering a sale, you save a ton of money on capital gains taxes.

For an extra sense of security in a deal like this, you can execute a *promissory note* to secure your investments. This is a written promise by one party to pay the other a specific sum of money. An alternative is a joint venture (JV) agreement, which clarifies all of the terms and conditions of the arrangement between the parties. Additionally, you can put all parties on the home insurance for more security. These types of agreements prevent anyone from getting any funny ideas—like running off with the money or property.

Let's take a look at how the specific profits would break down in my example. Nate gets eighty percent of the rental income every month, and will eventually get eighty percent of the profits when the property is sold. That's in addition to getting back his initial investment. Katie gets twenty percent of those same things, plus the tax incentive of paying a mortgage. So, what does that amount to in real numbers? Let's say the property cost $100,000, Nate puts down twenty percent, or $20,000. They rent it out for $1,600 a month, and after all operating expenses ($300 mortgage payment, property taxes, insurance, maintenance fees, etc.) the profit is $1,100 a month, to be split eighty-twenty between the two parties. After two years, Nate and Katie sell it for $160,000. The rental income for the two years they owned it was $26,400. After they pay off the remainder of the mortgage ($92,800, give or take, depending on the interest rate) and Nate takes back his initial investment ($20,000), they have $47,200 to split. Nate's share overall is eighty percent of that rental income ($21,120), plus eighty percent of the sale price ($37,760). Nate makes a total of $58,880 before taxes. Katie's twenty-percent share of the whole deal—not including the tax breaks she's gotten, especially if she lived there—is $14,720. Not bad for no money down. Katie has made enough money to put a down payment on another property, or to pay for a lease on a luxury car for two years. This is all without lifting a finger. This is one way to get creative, but the options are limitless.

5. Hard money: Hard-money loans are private loans from companies that don't require a good credit score or specific income. What's the catch? The down payment and the rates. Most of these lenders require that the borrower put down twenty-to-twenty-five percent of the purchase price up front. With hard-money loans, you pay only the interest on the loan every month and no money goes toward the principal, which is the original loan amount. The interest rates on these types of loans can be as high as thirteen percent—and here's the other big catch. The loan must be paid back in full after one year. This means that you must flip/sell the property at the one-year mark, or refinance it through a bank. Some people use hard-money loans to purchase an investment property, which they then fill with tenants. They use some of the monthly rental income to pay the interest on the loan, and set the rest aside for an actual down payment on a mortgage through a bank when the year is up. Anything is pos-

sible, but banks rarely deny applicants who can show that they have made a clear profit on their investment property for the year they've owned it.

JERRY'S TIPS ON FINDING THE RIGHT DEAL

- If the property is built on a slab or has foundation issues, walk away. Sometimes these things aren't that big of a deal, but other times they can suck all of the money out of your pockets.

- A *great deal* on the property is more important than the amount of your down payment. Put as little down as possible. After you put down whatever the bank requires you to, you only save $70 a month in payments for every $10,000 more you put down.

- If you buy a property with all cash, vacancies won't hurt as much as they will if you have a mortgage. Be sure to run the numbers and have six months of the property's operating expenses saved, just in case. Will your property be vacant for that long? Probably not, but better safe than sorry.

- Study the market around your property to make sure you aren't paying too much. DO NOT ASSUME THAT THE MARKET WILL APPRECIATE. ASSUME THAT IT WILL DROP FIVE TO TEN PERCENT AND OFFER THE SELLER THAT MUCH LESS.

- Anything that has been sitting on the market for more than 120 days should raise a red flag. That indicates a "cold market," and prices will probably drop five to ten percent. In a hot market, properties sit for no more than ninety days, presuming they are properly priced.

STEP 4. BEFORE YOU BUY, ASK YOURSELF THE FOLLOWING QUESTIONS:

- Is this worth buying and fixing up, or should I buy something similar and negotiate the price down to what I want to spend? (Remember, time is money; don't waste time.)
- Can I hold on to this and rent it so that it covers all expenses, in case it doesn't sell?
- What will I need to spend to make it great?
- What will I need to sell it for to make a profit?
- *Is this worth my time?*

STEP 5. VIEW THE PROPERTY.

Below are some questions that you must ask a seller. Use these to negotiate before and after an inspection. After the inspection is the best time to negotiate, because you have professionally obtained information about the property's problems and necessary fixes.

- Why are you selling?
- How much did you buy the property for?
- How long have you owned the property?
- Do you like the neighborhood?
- How old is the roof?
- Since you've owned the property, have you ever put on a new roof? (If they say no, ask for the previous owner's contact information and ask him or her the

same question. *If the roof hasn't been replaced for seven years or more, it's time for a new one! Factor this in when you negotiate the price.*

- How frequently do you have the furnace, hot water tank, and boiler serviced? (An encouraging answer is once a season.)
- Has a violent crime ever happened on or around the property? (In some states, it is required that the seller tell you if something criminal has occurred within a certain time span.)
- What do you hate about this property?
- When do you want to sell by?
- What are the local schools like (if it is a residential property)?

ADDITIONALLY, ASK YOUR REALTOR TO TRY TO GET THE FOLLOWING INFORMATION:

- How long has it been on the market?
- How many offers have been made and for how much?
- Have offers been turned down? Why?
- Have there been any offers accepted in the past? How long ago?
- How many times has the property fallen out of escrow? (The *escrow* period is the time between the signing of the purchase agreement and closing on the property.)

STEP 6. SUBMIT YOUR OFFER.

When you are ready to make a commitment, you have to submit a Purchase Agreement (PA). Your realtor or lawyer can create this. Keep in mind that this is where the art of negotiation begins. Along with your PA, you will need to provide an Earnest Money Deposit (EMD), which will be held in escrow (meaning the seller can't touch it) until closing and then applied to the purchase price. As I said earlier, though, you want to take steps to avoid losing your EMD if the deal goes south. Below, I outline how to prevent the loss of your deposit by using *contingencies.* You will also need Proof of Funds (POF), which is the proof that you have all of the cash you need to purchase the property, or a pre-approval letter from a bank that shows the seller you are getting the loan you need. Yes, you need both POF and EMD.

These are the contingencies you should try to include in your PA.

1. Due diligence contingency. This contingency allows you to back out of the deal if you are not satisfied once you do your due diligence/inspection. These contingencies usually expire on a certain date prior to closing, so be sure to stay on top of that and exercise it if necessary.

2. Physical inspection contingency, I'll go into more detail about physical inspections later, but the follow-

ing are typical physical inspections that you will want to have done on the property, and you'll want to be able to get out of your deal if they aren't satisfactory:

- General inspection
- Roof inspection
- Sewage inspection
- Foundation inspection
- Termite inspection
- Chimney inspection
- Environmental inspection
- Geological inspection

3. Financial/loan contingencies. I mentioned this earlier because it is *so* important. If you are intending to take out a bank loan to buy the property, you want a clause in your purchase agreement that says that if the loan doesn't come through, you get your EMD back and are completely off the hook. I have used finance contingencies on cash deals as well—in cases where I had most of the funds but was expecting the remainder before closing. In a case like that, my realtor and I explain that the finance contingency is in place just in case I am not able to come up with the remainder of the funds. If I can't, I want my EMD back so I can get out of the deal without consequence.

4. Concessions. When you close on a property, there are certain costs involved (fees to the bank's lawyers, etc). When I submit a PA, I usually ask for a percent-

age of those costs to be covered by the seller—these are *concessions*. I usually ask for three percent of the purchase price back as concessions; so, if I'm buying a one-million-dollar property, I ask for $30,000. I might not get it, but it doesn't hurt to ask.

5. The right to assign. This is one of my favorite things to put into a Purchase Agreement. It gives you the right to assign the property to someone else before you buy it. That's right: You can put this property under contract and if you have this contingency in place you can "sell" the property before buying it. For example, say I find a place for $100,000, negotiate it down to $70,000, and execute a PA to hold the property for thirty days. I include an inspection contingency and a finance/loan contingency. At that point, my realtor and I go look for someone to buy the property for $100,000. If we don't find anyone within thirty days, no problem, the property goes back on the market and we are protected thanks to the contingencies. If we do find a buyer, we make $20,000 without ever having touched the property or put out any money. Creativity.

6. Time-frame contingency. Time is money. You want to control the waiting game regardless if you're buying or selling. The last thing you want is for your offer to sit on the table for more than seven days. Depending on how motivated the seller is, I usually tell my realtor to let the seller know that my offer expires in five days—but I do it in such a way as to make someone

else the bad guy. What I mean is, I lay the blame for this contingency on an imaginary boss or another deal that is pending. I might say, "I need an answer in five days because I have only six days to make a decision on another property," or, "In five days my boss is going to take over these funds for another project." Blaming it on someone else prevents you from coming off as a jerk. Sellers want to feel good about the people they sell to, especially if they are discounting the property. The point of the time frame is that you want to be the one with the power in the negotiation, and that means controlling the timing.

STEP 7. DO YOUR DUE DILIGENCE/ INSPECTIONS.

Prior to conducting inspections on the property, obtain disclosure statements (these tell you about previous repairs or if a serious crime has taken place on the property) and permit history. Be sure that the permit history lines up with the current outline/floor plan of the property. For example, if the permit history shows two bedrooms are permitted but the current floor plan has three, this may mean that the third bedroom is not permitted. It's essential that all necessary permits for any additions or alterations were obtained by previous owners. Be sure that every bedroom has a closet. If it doesn't, then legally, the room is not a bedroom.

- As I mentioned, once the seller accepts your offer, but prior to closing on the property, you will want to have an inspector physically examine the property for problems.
- Some general inspectors also do foundation, sewage, termite, chimney, and roof inspections. Find an inspector that does all of these, so you won't have to hire a succession of specialized inspectors. In addition, be sure to walk the area in the morning, afternoon, and evening and chat with the neighbors and any tenants to get a feel for the neighborhood.
- Do not arrange for all inspections to be done at the same time. You do not want to order an environmental inspection, which is expensive and takes two to three weeks, before the general inspection—which is cheaper and quicker—is done to your satisfaction. This can save you a ton of cash.
- Find an inspector that also has experience doing construction. This way, as you are going through the inspection with him, you can ask specific questions. That's right, go with the inspector and take a pen and notepad. Whenever he points out a potential problem, ask these questions and note his responses.
    - Is it serious?
    - How much do you think it would cost to fix?
- You can use what you learned during the inspections to negotiate with the seller. You'll want the cost of any necessary repairs to come off of the purchase price. If

an inspector says something is broken, the seller can either fix it before you close or deduct the cost from what you owe. If the seller doesn't want to play ball, you can just walk away.

- Estoppel agreements and tenant information. Most people obtain an estoppel agreement only when they are buying an investment property with tenants already inside. This is a document that you obtain from the seller that identifies each tenant and provides some basic information about them, such as how much of a security deposit they have paid, how much they pay in rent, whether they've ever defaulted on their lease agreement, and more. One of the worst things you can do as an investor is buy a property with sketchy tenants or outright squatters. It is really difficult to evict tenants; it is expensive and a waste of time. Estoppel agreements, along with proper tenant screening moving forward, will reduce the chances that you'll need to deal with evictions. You can have a real estate attorney or realtor create a form estoppel agreement that can be executed for every tenant on the property. You'll also want to get copies of their leases, documentation of their security deposits, and copies of their personal IDs (driver's license or passport). I usually ask the seller for bank statements or receipts to show proof of the tenants past and present payments. Often, sellers let people live in the property rent free while they attempt to sell, to make it more attractive to buyers looking to purchase buildings that are at full capacity. Don't fall for this—especially if you are a new investor and need that rental income to make the numbers work.

- Condominium financials. If you are buying property as an investment, be sure that it's not a cooperative (co-op). Co-op properties are actually owned by a corporation and, as a buyer, you are purchasing shares in that corporation and receiving a proprietary lease. You are not actually buying the property outright. Some co-ops require board of director approval when buying/selling, which can be a disaster. Can you imagine if you had a cash buyer for your co-op but the board rejected him because he missed the credit score limit by one point? Please avoid this. Depending on the terms of the proprietary lease, co-ops can forbid you from renting out the property at all. Stick to condos and be sure that you can indeed rent them out. Usually, the Declaration of Covenants, Conditions, and Restrictions (CC&Rs) document will specify this information. When looking at the condo's financials, make sure that the building is not sucking down debt. The financials will tell you how much equity and liability the condo has, how much is in its reserve fund, and much more. Be sure that the building's equity outweighs its liability and that there is enough money in the reserves for rainy times. When you buy a co-op/condo, you are buying stock in the entire building.

- Walk-through. Be sure to do a full walk-through of the property right before closing, to assure that nothing has changed from when you did your physical inspections.

*Note: Steps 8 – 10 **apply to rental/investment properties only.***

STEP 8. FIND A GOOD MANAGEMENT COMPANY.

- I mentioned this earlier: If you are buying an investment property with tenants, you will want to hire a property management company to run the property. You do not want to act as a landlord, because a landlord is an investor who has lost his focus.
- Stay local when choosing a property manager.
- Identify your management company before closing, so that you can immediately hand responsibility for your properties over to it after closing.
- Do not pay more than ten percent of the rent per unit for your management company.

STEP 9. COLLECT YOUR PASSIVE INCOME EVERY MONTH.

STEP 10. REINVEST. DON'T. TOUCH. THE. CASH.

Reinvest your profits and you will be wealthy faster.

CHAPTER 6

INCOME FORM NO. 2 - STOCKS

People have been getting wealthy by owning and trading stocks and equities for a long time. There's just nothing like the stock market for long-term gains—but it takes patience and nerves of steel to be a player in this world. Stocks go up and down, but if you want to do well, you can't let market fluctuations scare you into selling—especially in a down market. You may have heard the tip, "Buy low and sell high," and I stand by it 100 percent. The problem is, it's difficult—if not impossible—to know how low *low* is and how high *high* is going to go. Many stocks have been considered *high* for ten years but they keep going up. So, I'd add that in addition to focusing on buying low and selling high, you have to focus on consistently adding to your portfolio every month. You have to get in and stay in for the long haul. It's a long game, and every person who has gotten rich in the market knows that.

Of course, there are times to consider liquidating your stocks: when you are about to retire, for example, and you need the cash to live on, or when you want to make other kinds of investments. But you're not going to want to do it all at once. If you know you want to retire, start thinking about selling off your stocks seven-to-ten years in advance. And if the market is crashing, try to put a hold on your plan; wait until the market comes back up and then sell. During this time, continue to put money in every month because, remember, when the market is low, you are getting the stocks at a discount. A *bear market* is when the stock market goes down thirty-to-sixty percent. The average bull/bear/bad market typically lasts about six-to-eight years. IF IT IS A BEAR/BAD MARKET DON'T SELL. This is when you want to be holding on to what you have and adding to it. When the market comes back, it will be even better than before it crashed.

Even when you retire and hit the beach, you want to keep some money in the market if you can—especially if you have enough that you can live off the dividends. *Dividends* are payments that you, as a stockholder, receive regularly from the company you've invested in. This money is your share of the company's profits, and is great passive income for you. By living off your dividends rather than selling your stocks, you are avoiding paying taxes on the sale.

Before the point when you are thinking about retirement, you should hold onto your stock at all costs (unless, as I said, you are planning to use the proceeds for another investment that will bring in even better returns). I repeat: Do not get rattled when the market goes down. The last time the market crashed, Warren Buffet, one of the greatest investors of all time, declared that he wouldn't dream of selling because he understood that, based on the last 200+ years of the market, he would ultimately come out on top. And he did. You have to stay the course.

To my elderly folks: Being indifferent to market fluctuations applies mainly to younger investors. When you are young and just getting into the market, you have a long horizon. It doesn't matter if the market wiggles around because it will eventually go back up. But if you are an older person who'd like to retire soon, and you have all of your money in stocks and the market drops a ton, that's a problem. You may not have the time to wait for it to go back up. So, the older you get and the closer to retirement, the more conservative your portfolio should be. You might want to keep more of your assets in cash or fixed-income instruments. I'm not an investment advisor, just here to offer an overview. When it comes time to make investment decisions, consult a professional who specializes in clients in your position, whether you are young or old.

Most people don't want to be wealthy because of the actual money, but because of what that money can buy them—namely, experiences and the time to enjoy them. Don't be afraid of stocks; be afraid of not understanding how to invest in them. And know this: Once you do understand the stock market, the best thing you can do is nothing. That's right, nothing. You don't have to manage your stocks daily. You definitely don't have to read the *Wall Street Journal* or watch the financial shows on TV; you don't even have to pick your own stocks.

I am going to show you how to set yourself up in the stock market so that you can build wealth for the long haul. These are strategies that schools don't teach but that have worked for rich people for hundreds of years.

Let's start by talking about dollar-cost averaging. Dollar-cost averaging, one of the best ways to benefit from the stock market, is when you put the exact same amount of money into your portfolio every month over a long period of time. I personally have the money automatically deducted from my bank account. I do it even before paying my bills, because I believe in *paying myself first*. Don't let that scare you. When the market drops, do not stop. That's right: Keep putting the same amount of money, or whatever you can afford, into your stock portfolio every month. You want to do this because, as I mentioned before, the lower the market goes, the cheaper you are getting the stock. And, because we now know the history of the stock market, we know that it will eventually go back up. Look at it as if you are getting the stocks on sale. When the price of the stock goes back up, your portfolio increases in value. I can't stress this enough: Don't let the dropping of the market scare you—be consistent. If you remain consistent, in ten to twenty years you will have made a lot of money overall. It will have multiplied. Trust me, you will thank me. Over time, your wealth will compound.

When buying stocks, what we are really buying is equity. *Equity* is simply when you own something or a piece of something. It can be a house, a stock, or a car. If you own it, it's equity. Equity is the only thing that makes a profit in the world.

In addition to dollar-cost averaging and staying in the market for the long haul, it is important to diversify your stock portfolio. This simply means don't put all of your eggs in one basket (your eggs being your money, of course). Do not put of all your money in one stock; rather, spread it out amongst different stocks. This creates a sense of balance in your portfolio and will reduce your chances of losing big-time. We are going to go over different stocks that you should be looking at. They are called *low-index funds.* Low-index funds are a way of owning the entire market. They are a way to make money and be safe at the same time.

> **JERRY FORD PRINCIPLE 5: WHEN PLAYING THIS GAME, NEVER COMPARE YOURSELF TO OTHERS. STRIVE ONLY TO DO BETTER THAN YOU DID THE DAY BEFORE. FOCUS ON BEING A BETTER YOU.**

THE FOUR PILLARS OF THE GAME

Let's talk about this game, the stock game. The way to win any game is to know the rules and strategies, practice, and play it better than everyone else. I used to love playing Super Mario Brothers. I could play that game for hours at a time as a kid, and the more I played it, the better I got. If you know the game, you know that you face the same obstacles each time you start over. Even as a child, I understood the benefit of this: I knew exactly what was coming next so I could prepare and adapt. Knowing what to expect made it possible for me to eventually beat the game. The game of stocks is very similar, but you don't want to keep starting over, because that would mean loss of cash. But you can learn from the experiences of others and begin to anticipate and prepare for what's to come. As Warren Buffett put it, "It's good to learn from your mistakes. It's better to learn from other people's mistakes." Allow me to help guide you along the road to wealth and begin to prepare you for the obstacles you'll face. Let me help you beat this game. To do that, I've developed a very easy-to-use guide: a manual of the stock market. I call it "The 4 Pillars of the Game"—the game being the stock market.

PILLAR 1. FACTS ABOUT THE GAME

- President Franklin Roosevelt created Social Security during the Great Depression. It was supposed to help older people. The bullshit about Social Security, at the time it was created, was that it didn't kick in until age sixty-five, but most people died at around age sixty-two. Today, we live longer *and* we can start collecting at sixty-two if we're willing to take a reduced benefit—which I don't recommend—but the odds are still against most people.
- Iatrogenic death, meaning death caused by the error of a doctor or hospital, is the third leading cause of death in America.
- The most amazing investors in the world are humble. They always do their homework and still admit that they could be wrong. Confidence is good; arrogance is dangerous.
- When a man with money meets a man with experience, the man with the experience ends up with the money and the man with the money ends up with experience.

- You can't get wealthy simply by working harder or putting in more hours. You have to make your money work for you.
- For over 100 years, people who invested in the stock market *and stayed with it* made the most money.
- The average cost of owning a mutual fund is 3.17 percent a year. Don't do it, unless you can get those fees down to to 1 percent or less.
- Owning the whole market with a low-cost index fund beats ninety-six percent of the mutual fund stock pickers over time. Low-cost index funds are affordable ways for investors to own all of the best performing stocks and bonds.
- A lot of studies show that, when it comes to stock picking, it's ninety-five percent luck and five percent skill. Don't pay fees for something that is ninety-five percent luck.

PILLAR 2. RULES OF THE GAME

- Find a good professional fiduciary (money manager) to help you manage your money and other assets—not a bank, because the fees will kill you. Use a referral.
- Buy low, sell high? Sure, but FOCUS ON LONG TERM.
- Don't pick individual stocks, buy only low-cost index. My favorites are:
  - S&P 500 (the biggest companies in the U.S.)
  - Russell 2000 IWM (it's a smarter stock)

- ◦ REIT's (a way to own real estate stock)
  - ◦ MSCI EAFE index for developed markets (e.g., Europe, Japan, Australia)
  - ◦ MSCI emerging markets index (e.g., China, Brazil)
- Buy for dividends.
- Don't trust stockbrokers. If they had the answers they would be sitting on a beach. These guys are salespeople masquerading as investors. It should be illegal.
- As a beginner, don't trade daily. Don't do anything. Let your money make money.
- Don't listen to anyone but your fiduciary/money manager. Don't open the *Wall Street Journal*. Don't listen to TV about stocks.
- When investing, do not pay more than 1 percent, or 100 basis points in fees, total!
- Take your emotions out of investing.
- Do dollar-cost averaging. (Remember, this is consistently putting the same amount of money into your portfolio every month.)

PILLAR 3. STEPS IN THE GAME

- Open a Fidelity or Schwab account (no banks; banks bet their money and all you can do is lose, not win. With a bank, you have no upside). You can open an account for FREE online or in an office; just Google them in your area.
- Buy low-cost index funds. See my favorites above.

DON'T LET THEM SELL YOU ANYTHING ELSE
BUT LOW-COST INDEX.

- Do dollar-cost averaging.
- DO NOTHING.

PILLAR 4. YOUR RESPONSE TO PEOPLE TRYING
TO CHANGE THE GAME SHOULD BE, "JUMP OFF
THE EMPIRE STATE BUILDING!"

- People: Invest with us, we can beat the market.
  - Response: Very few people beat the market, it's almost impossible.
- People: You have to take huge risks for huge rewards.
  - Response: "Rule No. 1: Never lose money. Rule No. 2: Never forget rule No. 1." —Warren Buffet

Warren Buffet believes that ninety percent of your stock investing should be in low-cost index funds.

FACTS YOU SHOULD KNOW ABOUT 401(K)S

A 401(k) is like contributing to a savings account you will be able to use after you retire. (You can withdraw the money sooner, but if you do, you'll pay steep penalties as well as the taxes you owe on the money. You don't EVER want to withdraw money from your 401(k) early, unless there is absolutely NO other option. Which means...never.)

There are two types of 401(k) plans: traditional and Roth. The most significant difference between them is that with a Roth 401(k), you don't pay taxes when you withdraw your money, as long as you follow all the rules. With a traditional 401(k), you DO pay taxes when you withdraw. So why doesn't everybody get a Roth 401(k)? They would if they could, but in order to qualify, your annual earnings must be under $130,000.

Some employers match the amount of money you invest in your 401(k) up to a certain amount, such as three percent of your paycheck, and that's more free money for you upon retirement. If your employer has a matching program, try to get the most out of it by investing at least as much as they are willing to match. It's a good feeling to watch your retirement account grow each month and know that part of it is a gift from your boss.

Depending on which type of 401(k) you have, every penny you put into the account is on a post-tax/pre-tax basis. And, keep in mind that you must keep the money in for a certain number of years or you will be penalized. Another catch is that 401(k) fees may be as high as four percent, which will devastate you in the long run. Below, I have provided the address of a website that outlines all of the hidden 401(k) fees. The bottom line is, always go Roth if you are eligible. To sum up:

- 401(k)s were not created to be your only source of income in retirement, but they certainly help.
- 401(k)s can charge up to four percent in fees. Don't be a victim of this. You can check to see how much you pay at: www.Americasbest401k.com or www.personalfund.com.
- If you make more than $130,000 per year, you cannot open a Roth 401(k), BUT, if you qualify, definitely open one or convert your regular 401(k) to a Roth. It allows you to pay taxes when the money goes into the account so that you don't have to pay them when you withdraw the money. In this world, taxes are going to keep rising; they are undoubtedly going to be higher at the time of withdrawal so you're better off paying them now. If you follow the requirements when withdrawing from your Roth 401(k) account, you will be able to withdraw "tax free." With a 401(k), the average employee gives up more than $140,000 in fees over his career if he makes around $30,000 a year and saves four to five percent of his pay per year. Someone making $95,000 a year loses almost $300,000!

"Benjamin Graham tells you to pick your stocks like you pick your groceries. I say, 'Bro I live in LA. Erewhon is expensive.'"

—JERRY FORD

CHAPTER 7

INCOME FORM NO. 3 – MONEY YOU EARN DAILY FROM YOUR JOB OR BUSINESS

In addition to discussing how to succeed at your "day job," this chapter explores ways to find happiness while mastering your human engineering skills. It's about how mental strength can help both your professional and private life.

MOVE UP IN YOUR COMPANY

How do we position ourselves to move up in our companies? Let's talk about leadership and happiness, because I believe that these play a huge role in our success. Dale

Carnegie said, "About fifteen percent of one's financial success is due to one's technical knowledge and about eighty-five percent is due to skill in human engineering, to personality and the ability to lead people." Throughout this chapter, I've incorporated different exercises for you to practice to help better position yourself to be successful in your career.

To move up in your company, being good at your job is a given. Doing your homework should be automatic. Being punctual and professional should be second nature. The technical part of your job is important and necessary, but you get zero cool points for this. This only makes you *good*. You want to be *great*. Most of your success will be based on how you deal with people and your ability to lead others—but people will only follow you if they like you. You have to be likeable. I'm not saying be cheesy, but being nice and smiling often is a start. The conversations that follow from a smile are limitless. Who knows? One smile at the right person might make you a million dollars or save your life. I'm not suggesting that you go around smiling at every person you see; that would be weird. I am simply suggesting that you smile more often.

Exercise: Smile at three different people you don't know every day for a week. If it makes a difference in your life somehow, add it to your daily routine.

Genuinely happy people are more likely to be successful and move up in their companies because they genuinely appeal to their bosses and customers. There are many ways to get people to like you without being fake or phony. The first way, and my personal favorite, is simply to remember their names. I know this sounds silly, but, as Dale Carnegie says, a person's name is one of the most important sounds to him. The next time you meet someone for the first time, say, a new boss or a potential business partner or investor, remember his name and two other things about him. Then, the next time you run into him, you can call him by name and ask specific questions about his life. This may very well make him think, "Man, that person is really thoughtful," and that can have real impact on your life. You've shown that guy you were paying attention to who he was and what he was saying—that you really care. The two facts can be as simple as remembering that he just had a kid and that he's a hardcore Dodgers fan. Remembering these simple things will help make him genuinely like you.

JERRY FORD PRINCIPLE 6: PEOPLE WHO ARE HAPPY ARE MORE LIKELY TO BE SUCCESSFUL, BECAUSE BOSSES AND CUSTOMERS GENUINELY LIKE THEM.

Exercise: The next time you're at an event or out meeting new people, make an effort to remember the name of each person you meet, as well as two facts about them. I'm not suggesting you ask someone deep, personal questions because that would be creepy. Just find out what interests him and ask questions such as, "Where are you from?" "Are you a sports fan?" Maybe you notice he is wearing a wedding ring; ask him how long he's been married, if he has any children, etc. The important thing is to learn and remember each person's name and two facts.

People love to feel important. They love to feel as if they're a part of something. When you meet someone, offer a compliment. Again, don't be creepy or come off as a flirt. Meet the person, observe something good about him, and comment on it in a kind way. Maybe he has on nice shoes or a nice suit. Tell him. Maybe he did something spectacular that you heard about. Congratulate him. Whatever it is, offer one genuine compliment. This will make him feel special—and it will make him like you.

People love to be part of a group; in fact, it's when we, as humans, are at our happiest. Synchronized movements relax us, make us happy, and make us feel important. Yoga, meditation classes, group discussions, prayer groups, mass, church services, even theatre performances are group settings in which people tend to be happy and relaxed. Being in groups unites us.

In order to evolve and become successful, you have to change the way you think. You have to work from the inside out, because success starts with you. You are who you are today because of your mindset from yesterday— but it is the way you think *today* that will define your future.

You have to help yourself before you can help someone else. Think about that long speech that flight attendants give on the plane, just before takeoff. (I know, nobody listens to that, but surely it has sunk in.) They always tell you to put your own oxygen mask on and secure it before you help others with theirs—even your own kids. This is because you can't fully commit to helping another person until you help yourself. It's the same way with business and financial success.

Two practices that can change the way you think:

1. Meditation
2. Cognitive Therapy

Meditation helps prevent stress and silence our thoughts so we can find peace. We don't realize how restless our minds are until we check in, which is why it is so important to meditate. I challenge you to sit down or lay down on your back once a day for five to ten minutes. Choose a quiet place, turn your phone and all other devices off, and meditate. Close your eyes. Try not to focus on anything but your breath. Breathe in through your nose and out through your mouth. Your mind may want to drift, and that's OK; just continue to bring the focus back to your breathing and relax. Don't worry if this is hard to do at first. Like anything else, the more you practice, the better you get at it.

Cognitive therapy is another way to change your customary thought process. It's a therapy designed to help you let go of negative thought patterns about yourself or others. There are many ways to exercise cognitive therapy, but the goal is to keep negative thoughts out of your mind. This is important, because if you don't catch those negative thoughts fast enough, they can stick in your subconscious and affect your body and actions in concrete ways. Negative thought patterns can cause you to treat yourself and others badly. They can make you ugly.

Exercise: Whenever a negative thought enters your mind, stop, acknowledge that it's there, and write it down or take a mental note. After taking that note, physically tear it up—or think about tearing it up—and trash it. Be the master of your thoughts, or they may become the master of you.

Meditation and cognitive therapy mitigate stress, and that can help prevent mental disorders. Did you know that mental illness is one of the top three diseases affecting people today? It's killing us. Change the way you think. Meditate, address your problems, and rest your mind.

I'm sure you're aware that physical exercise is beneficial to your health and happiness as well. People who exercise regularly are generally happier and less likely to suffer from depression or other mental disorders. Studies done all over the world have shown that people who walk, cycle, run, garden, etc., derive mental-health benefits from these activities. Research also indicates that people with sedentary jobs are more likely to get cardiovascular disease than those who stand while working.

Exercise: I challenge you to walk, run, cycle, or do any other form of exercise for forty-five minutes a day, at least three days a week. Did you know that simply walking at your own pace for this period of time, three days a week, improves your mental function and helps prevent premature aging? Do it. I further challenge you to do as many of these workouts or walks outdoors as possible. The weight room and the treadmill are great, but the outdoors is amazing for stress relief. I personally like to mix it up and exercise both indoors and outside in nature.

JERRY FORD PRINCIPLE 7: BE LIKABLE, BE GREAT AT LEADING, AND BE GREAT AT DEALING WITH PEOPLE.

START YOUR OWN BUSINESS

As I stated earlier, it doesn't matter if you work for a company with hundreds of people or are a one-man shop, these concepts will be of use to you. They apply if you are an artist, trainer, doctor, massage therapist, or employee of a Fortune 500 company.

FOUR BENEFITS OF STARTING YOUR OWN BUSINESS

1. **There is no limit to where you can go.** When it comes to starting your own business, there is absolutely no limit to how far you can go. You may start out as a small business and be successful that way, or end up growing into a major corporation. The choice is yours. You get to choose how far you want to take your enterprise, and the only person who can stop you is the one in the mirror: you.

2. **As a business owner, you are four times more likely to become a millionaire.** This is your company, which means you control how it operates. You control the partners, the employees, the salaries, and the split. You control when you start working and when you stop. You control the decisions being made. You get the tax write-offs and you can reap whatever benefits you choose. Your company is your baby, and you are four times more likely to become a millionaire than if you were employed at someone else's company.

You don't learn this in school, and your bosses will never tell it to you because they want you working for them, making them rich, not yourself. Stop making others rich while you do the heavy lifting and save pennies from every paycheck. You will never get wealthy by working longer hours and saving an extra nickel or dime.

I'm not saying quit your job, because that would be impractical. You need your income from it until your business takes off. I'm simply saying start your business *while* working at your day job. Remember my use of time-blocking when I was trying to fit in my daily allotment of reading? Time-blocking can be used for starting a business, as well. Start off by putting "my company" or "my business" into your calendar for thirty minutes or even one hour a day, and during those timeslots, work on it. Maybe the first week you brainstorm and write down ideas. Maybe the second week you start drafting a business plan (you can find samples online). Don't let the fear of being wrong or having silly ideas stop you from starting. In a few weeks' time, you may be using those blocks of time to start executing your plan. The most important moment in any enterprise is when you start it. Time-block your business and make it happen. Own your own business.

People are so caught up in the supposed "security" of

working for others that they don't realize it can be the riskiest thing of all. You want a steady income, a reliable gig, benefits; but if you look at the numbers, you'll conclude that the only true security is in working for yourself. Of the original Fortune 500 companies from 1954, only fourteen percent are still in business. This means that a lot of people lost their jobs well before retirement. You need only open the paper to see the way downsizing and layoffs have swept the country over the past ten years, for a wide variety of economic, technological, and other reasons. Employment just isn't as safe and secure as you think—unless you are your own boss.

3. **Be the boss.** There are a lot of benefits to being your own boss, but my personal favorite is that you can make your own schedule, meaning that you can spend time doing what's most important to you. How many times have you had to cancel that vacation with your family because your boss needed you to work? How many times have your boss's requests gotten in the way of your relationships with friends or loved ones? Think about it.

Work itself, regardless of whether you have your own business or work for someone else, can crowd out other important aspects of life if you don't prioritize what's important at important times. Although being a boss involves a lot of responsibility, not having a boss to answer to brings with it a kind of freedom: freedom to take that vacation, go to that game or event with your kids, or enjoy that special time with those who are important.

4. **Leave behind a legacy.**

   ◦ When you die, what will people have to say about you?
   ◦ What do you want to leave behind for your family?
   ◦ What do you want your obituary to say?

When you think about these things, you are contemplating your legacy. Valuing your legacy means optimizing your life right now—so that what you leave behind is worthy of who you want to be.

Exercise: I want you to write down the answers to the legacy questions above and I want you to start living in a way that is in tune with those answers. Now, envision your ideal obituary. What would it say (besides, "He died in his sleep of very, very old age")? If you want your obituary to say that you were determined, a great person, and helped others, then you need to become determined, focused, and start doing notable good deeds. If you want it to say that you left a successful business behind, start building that successful company.

You have the choice to build your legacy now, so that your loved ones from generation to generation can benefit from it and extend it. Build a company that can continue to operate and grow without you. Truly great companies, such as Apple, Microsoft, Coca Cola, Target, and many others, have continued to grow well beyond the lifespan of their founders. Your legacy starts now.

FIVE THINGS YOU NEED TO START A SUCCESSFUL BUSINESS

1. A MENTOR

- Hang out in places where you can possibly find a mentor in your field. Successful people tend to hang out in places like luxury restaurants/lounges, luxury gyms, the golf course, or at professional seminars. If you don't live near these types of places, don't worry. Drive, Uber, or take the bus to one of these places once a week. Put yourself in a position to meet successful people. It can be scary, but sometimes all you have to do is change your environment to begin changing your life. Being in the right place at the right time is a major component of success. Having the right attitude is the final piece. Get comfortable with being uncomfortable and you will grow faster than you can imagine. Be willing to evolve.
- Pick a successful person—then get to know him. Asking someone to be your mentor can feel a bit weird to both

parties. There's something about the word *mentor* that is off-putting—but you can get past that. First of all, don't say, "Will you be my mentor?" Once you've identified someone, simply offer to buy him dinner or coffee in exchange for answering a few questions. He will most likely say yes. Everyone likes to hear himself talk, and successful people *love* it. For a truly fruitful relationship, you have to make the person *want* to mentor you. As Dale Carnegie put it, you have to "bait the hook to suit the fish"—in other words, make him feel special and eager to work with you. Here are some tips:

- Be easy going and in a good mood.
- Establish the relationship slowly. The first week, maybe just say hi. The second week, ask how his week is going. The third week, engage him in a conversation about investing or sports—and so on. Get him to like you in all of those ways we discussed earlier in the chapter.
- Ultimately, ask him how his business is going.
- Listen.
- Compliment him on his success, e.g., "You really inspire me to want be half as successful as you are. You're a genius." Keep your compliments genuine. (You obviously admire him, or you wouldn't want him for a mentor.)
- Once you have gotten him to agree to dinner or coffee, chat him up about how he started out and progressed along his path to success.

- Try to set up a regular time to meet. If he can't commit to this, tell him you'll email him the following week and ask for his email address. (If he offers his phone number, even better, but don't ask for it.) If he refuses to give you his contact information or says he's too busy to meet with you—or even if he just seems hesitant—say, "I totally understand; let me know if you are ever free." This person may not be your mentor after all. That's OK. Keep moving.
- Read books. Reading books is one of my favorite ways to seek out mentors. The authors of the books I choose to read are among my chosen mentors even if I never get a chance to meet them. Although human-to-human interaction is best, reading someone's book is an effective way to learn from him—and this means that the number of mentors you have can be limitless.

From there, you can get creative: Start a book club with friends, where you all read a page or a chapter of an influential book and discuss it. You will be surprised at what you learn from an open discussion among motivated individuals. Always be open to learning and seeing things from the next person's point of view. You can do this through a technique I call the LAD Technique: Listen, Analyze, Decide. The LAD Technique can help you in life and business. Never reject information simply because you don't like the person it comes from or point-of-view it represents. The idea is to listen to the information first, analyze it for validity, and only then decide if you agree or disagree, and how it might affect your life.

2. A "CLEAN" IDEA THAT SOLVES PEOPLE'S PROBLEMS

The first thing to do when you come up with an idea is to wash it ten times—i.e., clean it. What I mean is, go over it ten times, each time with fresh eyes. Then pick ten of the smartest, most successful people you know and ask each of them to review and critique your idea. Be sure to pick people who will be 100 percent honest with you.

When you first come up with an idea, it can seem good. But you have to give other people a chance to rip it apart, shake it down, ask the hard questions, and ultimately wash the dirt out of it. It might hurt a little, but it's better if the criticism comes from trusted friends and mentors than the world at large. You want your idea to be in perfectly clean condition before you introduce it to the world. You only get one chance to make a first impression, and it can either destroy your efforts or help you build them into something life-changing.

As each person you've selected washes the dirt off your idea, be sure to be open to what he is saying and why he is saying it. You may not agree with everyone, but that doesn't mean the process is a waste of time. Use my LAD technique, take what makes sense, and leave the rest. At the end of the process, you should have a "clean" idea that's ready for the world.

3. RARE AND VALUABLE SKILLS IN YOUR FIELD, PER THE "TEN TIMES RULE"

If you haven't already developed the specific skills required for your idea to succeed, start now and practice as if your life depends on it. If this means additional years in school, getting a certification, or gaining experience, so be it. Regardless of whether you are a beginner or advanced, I want you to ask yourself if you are a master at these skills. You have to be the best. You have to be a master because being good is not good enough. Everyone is good. You have to be so good that no one can deny you. The only way to reach master status in anything is to practice, practice, practice, and practice. I want you to practice so hard that when you actually perform, it's easy because it's second nature.

"If you train hard the fights will be easy, but if you train easy the fights will be hard."

—JERRY FORD

One definition of being a master at something—my definition—is practicing ten hours per day for ten years.

This is a total of 87,600 hours. If ten years seems like too much time to devote to anything, fine—just practice for 87,600 hours.

Don't run away just yet. I'm not telling you that you won't be successful unless you practice this long, I'm telling you to practice enough that no one can deny how good you are. Practice until you physically and mentally can't anymore, and then do it for an additional hour. Trust me, if you do this, you will dance circles around your competition.

4. THE RIGHT TEAM

Get the right people on the bus and in the right seats. Getting the right team in place for your business is life or death. Getting the right team in the right positions in your company is just as important. Over seventy percent of startups fail because they lack capital and don't have the right team. Sometimes the company *does* have the right team, but still fails because the players are not in the right positions. Having the ideal team in the ideal spots is key. Can you imagine a basketball team where LeBron was playing Center, Shaq was playing Point, Kareem was shooting, Kobe was a Forward, and Michael Jordan was the other Forward? That team—consisting of some of the best players in the NBA—would probably lose badly because the players' positions weren't a good fit. If you get the right team *and* put people in their best spots, you will have a strong shot at success.

The great thing about an all-star team is that even if your guys take a wrong turn, and they probably will, they will quickly find their way back onto the right track. Additionally, you don't have to manage an all-star team, you just have to lead and coach them. An all-star team manages itself as you lead them to victory. The only person you need to manage is yourself.

5. EFFECTIVE MARKETING

Having an amazing product or service is a great thing, but it doesn't mean much if people aren't talking about it. Yes, *talking*—because word-of-mouth is your number-one best marketing tool. Potential customers are much more likely to take a suggestion from someone they trust than pay attention to a paid advertisement any day. Add to that the fact that paid advertising is expensive! Do not make the mistake of putting a lot of your capital into conventional marketing—even if you have a healthy budget. You are better off putting most of your money into the product or service, to make it the best it can be, and then letting its quality speak for itself.

So, how do you generate word of mouth? Simple. Be SO GOOD at what you do that your clients can't stop talking about you. For example, I am a trainer and the following are some of the things that I do to keep my clients satisfied, talking about me, and coming back for more. Some of these are specific to my job, but I'm sure you can see how they might apply to your enterprise as well.

- I'm always early. I'm there and ready to start before the client arrives, so as not to waste his or her time.
- I give my clients my all for every second of the session and never shortchange them—but I don't complain if they need to cut a session short.
- I treat each session as if it were the first one we've ever had together. We all bring our best game early on, when we are trying to impress a client or customer. I try to carry that attitude over into every session and I never take a long-time client for granted. In fact, I value my loyal clients most highly of all!
- I'm always clear on what the client needs to do to reach his or her goal and what I, as the trainer, can (or can't) do to make that happen—so that there are no surprises. I am very honest when talking about goals and time frame.
- I give my clients what they ask for and more, if possible.
- I diagnose and then prescribe.
- I kill the noise—meaning that I kill any negative vibes I might be giving out before seeing clients. They can sense when I'm dealing with my own stuff, and nobody wants to work with someone who's not in a positive, can-do frame of mind.

- When my clients come in, I ask them how they are feeling, emotionally and physically. The way a client feels on a given day may alter my plan for his or her workout. Every session is tailored not only to the person, but to the person *in that moment.* It's up to me to adapt to moods, physical injuries, illnesses, whatever is going on.
- I always ask my clients about their work and families because (A) these things are the major cause of stress in people's lives, and (B) it gets them talking and makes them more comfortable. When my clients feel comfortable with me, they are happy—and happy people get better results faster. Besides—we all like to hear ourselves talk.
- I never forget that I work for my clients. I don't volunteer personal information unless they ask, and that includes the ones I consider friends. And if they do ask, I am careful not to get distracted from the workout because I'm talking. I don't stop counting or giving instruction. For as long as the session lasts, it's all about the client, and it is up to me to provide him or her with my undivided attention.
- I continue to count aloud, even if it's in a low voice, when they are telling me a story. Every once in a while, I reassure them that I'm listening—but the workout is my main focus, since that is what they are paying me for.
- I compliment my clients when they are doing a good

job and correct them when they lapse into bad form, while always trying to stay positive and encouraging. People want to know what they are doing wrong—but they especially want to know when they are doing well.

- I always put the weights into my clients' hands and take them out when they're done with them. This is to help them save their energy, and I tell them so.

- I have a profile set up in my iPhone, backed up on my iCloud, for each client, so that I can take notes. After a session, I write down what they did well, what they can improve on, what we worked on, and how they felt. This helps me help them improve, and it shows them that I care. I even ask them about anything that might have bothered them after the previous session and alter the workout accordingly, while keeping track of their progress.

- I give my clients every twenty-fourth session free. I don't advertise this, but announce it at the beginning of the session, treating it like a "random act of kindness." This creates the spirit of reciprocity. In other words, it makes my clients want to do something nice for me in return.

- I'm responsive and understanding. If a client really hates a particular exercise, I find another way to work that muscle.

- I use my words. Studies have shown that the majority of people do not like to be touched during workouts. Instead of pushing or prodding them, I explain or demonstrate on myself, and only touch a client with verbal permission and as a last resort (except when I'm stretching them, of course).

- I always deliver on my promises. If I tell a client I will make him look good in a bathing suit in time for his vacation, I do my part to make that happen. (Of course, he has to do his part as well!)
- Unless they specifically ask me to, I don't yell to motivate my clients. Most people hate to be yelled at, and prefer an occasional "almost," "you can do it," "you got this," or "just five more." A firm, energized, positive tone provides the best motivation of all.
- I always wear a watch to keep time for timed exercises—but I never let the client see me checking it as if I am bored or impatient.
- I look presentable in my fitness clothes.
- I apologize—sometimes even in situations where I know I'm right. In case of a conflict, my clients are always right. If a client complains or contradicts me about something, I silently check in with myself to see if he has a point. If he does, I try to fix the problem. If he's wrong, I try to fix it anyway! (Remember my story about Bill and you'll understand the ultimate value of deferring to the client.) When my clients are not getting results, I say, "You are doing well—but let's add XYZ to our plan." That XYZ might be something they were supposed to do all along, but instead of criticizing, I just compliment and suggest.

- I reassure my clients that we are a team, and together we will get them to their goal.

Thanks to her hard work with me, Alisha Boe—the actress best known for the popular Netflix series *Thirteen Reasons Why*—is in the best shape of her life.

I'm proud to train DJ Mobeatz, Big Sean's official DJ. We travel all over the world together when he's on tour.

In 2018, under my supervision, top model Amelia Gray safely lost twenty pounds in thirty days. The inspiration came from me, but the determination was all hers.

Dutch TV anchor and presenter and former cycle-racer Danielle Oerlemans has four kids, but she never misses one of her daily 5:30 a.m. training appointments. She's a beast!

French model Pierre Abena and I go hard! It's no crime that we like to relax a little after our sessions.

Adam Drawas, the co-owner of Walker Drawas Public Relations Agency, works out with me six days a week. He is always summer ready.

Business travel is no excuse for missing a workout. I train Camilo Becdach, a partner at McKinsey & Company, five days a week via Skype, no matter where he is in the world—no exceptions!

Maybe none of the above sounds like "marketing," as you understand it—but I assure you, being good at what you do is the best marketing plan of all. Here are some additional marketing tips:

- Your product or service will never be for everyone, so don't waste time mass marketing. Pick a few different audiences, market to them specifically, and measure the results. Don't try to create a product for everyone, because that's pretty much impossible. Instead, put your energy into figuring out who would be interested in what you are selling, make them aware of it, and do what you can to get them excited about it. When they come on board, reward them.
- Copy. It's OK to copy what other companies are doing, if it works. This applies to both the product and the marketing—but within legal bounds, of course. Do what they did, then make it better!
- Adapt to the times. As hard as it might be for some of us to accept, social media is where most people get their information these days, and online is where they go to get recommendations, read reviews, and shop. You have to have a presence online—and a positive one—or you really don't exist. Create a website for your business and a page on every social media platform you know of—especially Instagram, Facebook, and Twitter. All this is a lot of work, so I would suggest hiring someone to manage your social media and website. As little as $50-$100 a month can take care of it and keep users engaged. These days, social

media can make you a lot of money, if you know how to use it. And that means providing people with genuine content, not just ads and self-promotion. Forget the hard sell—if you put great information out there, people will trust what you have to offer and seek out your services.

There are people out there—celebrities, mainly—who have so many followers on social media that they are considered "influencers." Their attention can actually be had—for a price. If you think this is worth it, go ahead and look into it, but it'll cost you. Here are a few prominent people's prices per social media post, according to Hopper HQ:

- Selena Gomez makes $550,000 per post
- Kim Kardashian makes $500,000 per post
- Cristiano Ronaldo makes $400,000 per post
- Kylie Jenner makes $400,000 per post
- Kendall Jenner makes $370,000 per post
- Khloe Kardashian makes $250,000 per post
- Kourtney Kardashian makes $250,000 per post
- Cara Delevingne makes $150,000 per post
- Gigi Hadid makes $120,000 per post
- LeBron James makes $120,000 per post

Be innovative with your marketing. Be creative. Don't be safe, be bold.

CHAPTER 8

LOAD, AIM, AND EXECUTE

Now that you've begun to amass the knowledge you need to get started on building wealth, the most important part awaits you. The most important part of attaining the three forms of income is *execution*. Lots of people have the knowledge, but knowledge without execution means nothing. Knowing how to get wealthy alone will not turn into its physical equivalent. You have to DO. You have to take a chance and jump. Knowledge is power, but execution is key. Don't wait or hesitate, because waiting can become a habit. Waiting will keep you on the bench of life while the game goes on without you.

Once you have taken the time to prepare, done your home-work, and cleaned your idea to the max, execute as quickly as possible. Think about a snake. It moves slowly around its target doing its homework, sizing up the opponent.

Then, when it's ready, it strikes like lightning. The snake strikes fast because it cannot afford to miss. It knows by instinct that it may not get a second chance at its prey. For the snake, speed of execution is a matter of life or death. For you, speed of execution is a matter of the life or death of your business endeavor.

WHY IS THIS INFORMATION IMPORTANT?

I believe that everyone deserves an equal shot at the tools and knowledge of wealth-building. In reality, that isn't the case—and that's one reason why I wrote this book. I'm handing you the knowledge, but it's your choice to take it in and use it to change your life.

Financial literacy is not commonly taught in public schools, but it should be. There is so much money in the world and countless ways to get your share of it. Sadly, most of it remains in the hands of very few people. It is up to the rest of us tap into the wealth stream. I used to wonder why there are so few billionaires in this world, while the majority of the population is poor or lower class. What are those billionaires doing differently from the rest of us with their twenty-four-hour days? What I realized was that we might all have the same amount of time to accomplish things, but we don't all have the same level of financial literacy. And that knowledge, as I've stated, is key to success. By putting this book filled with specialized knowledge in your hands, I am trying to help you solve that problem. I'm outlining for you the major ways that people have built wealth for ages.

Now, let me also help you solve the execution problem. Let this book inspire you to make that jump and take that chance, regardless of how old or young you are. It's never too late to pursue wealth. Oprah Winfrey was between jobs and over thirty before she made it big. Robin Thicke didn't have his first hit record until he was thirty. Martha Stewart's first cookbook wasn't published until she was forty-one. Viola Davis didn't become a household name until she was cast in the film *The Help* at age forty-six. It's not too late for you to start climbing the ladder to success.

Let's look at this from another direction. Regardless of your past or where you are in your life, just know that you can start fresh right now and take control of what happens tomorrow. I'm not saying that what you did yesterday won't affect your future; I'm saying don't let yesterday push you into a dark corner. Don't let yesterday make you feel like tomorrow has to be the same. Today, *right now, right this second,* you can choose to change and make better decisions for tomorrow.

CHAPTER 9

THE BIG DAWGS

I have interviewed some of the coolest and most successful people from all industries, in order to get snapshots
of their portfolios and investment strategies for you. My
subjects included finance experts, artists, corporate busi-
nesspeople, and other entrepreneurs. My goal was to
provide you with the inside scoop on what the people that
we strive to be like are investing in, and why. Because I
wanted concrete answers and not just vague notions, I
asked each of them, if they had $100, how would they
invest it? I chose the figure of $100 because it is in reach
of even the most cash-strapped potential investor. Anyone
can scrape together $100; the question is what to do with
it. Without further ado, I welcome you to the Big Dawgs.

BILL

Expertise – Retired investor

What does your portfolio look like or what are you invested in?

Cash, oil, and real estate.

What percentage of your money is invested in each area?

The majority of my wealth is in cash, followed by oil and then real estate.

If you had $100, how would you invest it?

All in select oil.

SHAYAN AFSHAR

Expertise – Jeweler and watch dealer

What does your portfolio look like or what are you invested in?

Real estate, watches, crypto currency, and the stock market.

What percentage of your money is invested in each area?

Eighty percent in real estate, five percent in watches, two-and-a-half percent in the stock market (AAPL stock).

If you had $100, how would you invest it?

The entire $100 into AAPL stock. It's a great long-term hold and I do not see them failing.

LUKE CHRISTOPER

Expertise – Rap artist (recording and writing)

What does your portfolio look like or what are you invested

in?

Real estate and cash.

What percentage of your money is invested in each area?

Forty percent in real estate and sixty percent cash.

If you had $100, how would you invest it?

The entire $100 in products or merchandise to resell.

JOSEPH JOHNSON

Expertise – Investor/urban development

What does your portfolio look like or what are you invested in?

Small business, real estate, and stocks.

What percentage of your money is invested in each area?

Seventy percent in small business, twenty percent in real estate, and ten percent in stocks (Target, blue chip, S&P 500).

If you had $100 how would you invest it?

Seventy dollars in small business, twenty dollars in REIT's/ real estate, and ten dollars in stocks that pay dividends.

CAMILLO BECDACH

Expertise – Management consultant/partner (strategy for Fortune 500 companies)

What does your portfolio look like or what are you invested in?

Mix of investment funds, both long- and short-term risk.

What percentage of your money is invested in each area?

All in blind investment funds.

If you had $100 how would you invest it?

All in risky, long-term investment funds.

DJ MOBEATZ

Expertise – DJ and music producer

What does your portfolio look like or what are you invested in?

Cash, Crypto currency, and the stock market.

What percentage of your money is invested in each area?

Eighty-two percent in cash, sixteen percent in crypto, and two percent in oil.

If you had $100 how would you invest it?

Buy items to resell on websites/apps like eBay or Offer Up. It takes a little research, but you can buy this stuff for a lower price and resell it higher fairly easily. This is a low-cost method for turning profit so that you can make larger investments.

WHITNEY JOHNS

Expertise – Fitness trainer/nutrition expert

What does your portfolio look like or what are you invested in?

My own online fitness app (Fit with Whit).

What percentage of your money is invested in each area?

Ten percent in cash and ninety percent in Fit with Whit.

If you had $100 how would you invest it?

All in my online fitness platform.

J. MALLORY MCCREE

Expertise – Actor and expert in the business of acting

What does your portfolio look like or what are you invested in?

Myself as an artist (I own a production company and a tech company and produced a short film) and stocks.

What percentage of your money is invested in each area?

Fifty percent in the business of acting, twenty-five percent in the production company, fifteen percent in the tech company, and ten percent in stocks.

If you had $100 how would you invest it?

In film production equipment and in creating opportunities rather than waiting for them.

These days I, Jerry Ford, do not acquire liabilities out of pocket. I only acquire assets, then make them pay for my liabilities. I love Rolexes, Tom Ford suits, and nice cars. I love flying first class, wearing gold and nice clothes, and shopping when I feel like it. I love buying my mom whatever she wants and contributing to my brother's music business. I love buying gifts because I like doing nice things for people. Studies show that the satisfaction you get from doing something nice for someone else lasts a lot longer than the satisfaction you get from doing something for yourself. I love to give—but I don't pay for most of the things I acquire and give away; my assets do. Again, *the difference between the rich and the poor is that rich people buy assets and poor people buy liabilities and convince themselves that they are assets.* I want you all to acquire assets and equity and let them pay for the liabilities that you want.

"Those who are crazy enough to think they can change the world usually do."

—STEVE JOBS

CHAPTER 10

LETTER TO BLACK AMERICA

Dear Family,

I know I told you this book was going to be about how to amass wealth—and I've stuck to the subject throughout most of it. I hope I've given you a lot of concrete tools to begin your new financial journey. But now I want to broaden my context and speak about a larger matter that we as African Americans face. I want to talk about the way racism has an impact on opportunity, so that you can push hard against it and succeed in spite of it.

First of all, don't be manipulated. Don't let anybody manipulate you into doing anything you don't want to do, especially negative things. Don't let anyone tell you what is not possible because anything is. There's only one person who can stop you, and that's the person in the mirror. It doesn't matter who you are, where you've been, or where you are at, you can do anything and anything is possible for tomorrow.

One of my favorite books of all time is *The New Jim Crow*, by Michelle Alexander. This book talks about mass incarceration in America, and how today it's legal to discriminate against criminals the same way it was once legal to discriminate against blacks. Slavery is still in effect, Alexander points out, but it has taken a new form. Mass incarceration and discrimination against people who have been put into the system—mainly people of color—constitute "the new Jim Crow."

Sure, slavery itself may be illegal now, but pay attention to the elephant in the room by looking a bit more closely at our legal system. Slaves, in addition to the horrible oppression and abuse they suffered, had no voting rights and were denied education and economic opportunities. They were denied their basic human, legal, and moral rights. Well, guess what? Nowadays, anyone with a criminal record is treated the same way. Anyone who has served time in a correctional facility, no matter how unfair his trial or how trivial his crime, is considered a criminal and denied his civil rights. You don't need to look hard to see that the majority of these "criminals" are African American.

This entire group of people has become enslaved, facing

employment restrictions, housing restrictions, denial of voting rights, denial of educational opportunity, denial of social services such as food stamps and welfare—in short, all of their rights as Americans. Racism in America has not ended. The enslavement of a race hasn't ended. The name has just been changed from *slave* to *criminal*.

For as long as America has existed, those in power have tried to manipulate us by telling us that we were less than human and didn't deserve equal rights. They have criticized us for having a drug problem while covering up the fact that the CIA was helping to get us hooked. The CIA has now admitted that in 1998, U.S.-backed guerilla armies in Nicaragua were smuggling crack into the U.S. Guess where the drugs ended up? In black neighborhoods. It's safe to say that the CIA was a major cause of the crack epidemic—but it is the populations of our cities that have suffered for it. And continue to suffer.

Black America, you need to know this. Between 1980 and 2001, the African American prison population jumped from 350,000 to 2.3 million. Shocking, right? But what that statistic doesn't reveal is the reason: It isn't that behavior in black communities has changed, it's that the laws have changed. They tell us that blacks abuse drugs in the greatest numbers but that just isn't true. For the past forty years, only fifteen percent of drug users were black; whites were by far the majority.

Black America, you need to know this. Blacks who kill whites get the death penalty eleven times more often than whites who kill black people. Not only that: Blacks are more than six times as likely to go to jail for the same crime, no matter what it is. They tell us that ninety-three percent of blacks are killed by other blacks, but what they don't tell us is that eighty-four percent of whites are killed by other whites. They tell us that blacks are dangerous, but what they don't tell us is that blacks committed only thirty-six percent of violent crimes while whites committed forty-two percent. (These FBI statistics are from 2015.)

Black America, take a close look at how they've set up minimum jail sentences for crack vs. powdered cocaine. It takes twenty-eight grams of crack cocaine to get you a minimum five-year sentence, while it takes 500 grams of powdered cocaine to get you the same. Based on that, can you guess which race of people is associated with each drug? You got it. The result is, the punishment of blacks is eighteen times more severe than that of whites. (It used to be 100 times worse, but President Obama reduced it to eighteen-to-one. Who knows where we're going now?)

Black America, you need to know this. They say that we abandon our kids more than anyone else, but what they don't say is that studies show that black men who don't live with their kids are more likely to keep in contact with them than any other race. They say that we should shout,

"All lives matter," but American history continues to ignore black history. How can they leave out an entire race, especially when we were enslaved for 400+ years? We say, "Black lives matter" because we need to be recognized and we want to be treated fairly. We want cops to stop executing African Americans without consequence and we want justice for the ones that have killed us.

Our legal system's track record makes it clear: black America is seen as unequal to white America. Black America, you need to know that "redlining"—a common practice where banks deal unfairly with people of color when it comes to mortgages, insurance, and other services—has been responsible for huge losses of black wealth for decades, as well as the de facto segregation of neighborhoods by race.

I write this letter to you because I want to be a source of specialized information that can change your life. I invite everyone, but especially my black brothers and sisters, to build wealth with me and continue to break the barriers that still stand against us. I invite you to become knowledgeable with me and become part of a movement of African American wealth-building. Let's be role models for the generations coming up behind us. Let's take calculated risks. Let's jump.

As a black man, as a person from the ghetto, I was told

many times that I would end up dead or in jail. Well, I did end up in jail, but I didn't let that form who I was or be the last chapter of my story. I chose to live a different life, to seek knowledge, become knowledge, and become great at what I wanted to do. I sought out opportunity and jumped at it.

Those who said they knew my story were wrong. Don't let anyone say they know your story, when it is still to be written. They get mad at us when we don't salute the American flag, or don't sing along to the national anthem. That flag and song symbolize a patriotic country, they tell us, "the home of the free." We are expected to exhibit national loyalty, to embrace a doctrine of equality and love. But—at least right now—that doctrine is a fantasy. The actions of our white leaders and fellow citizens speak for themselves.

America is the only country in the world whose laws cast out an entire race. White law enforcement continues to murder and persecute minority citizens. Racist acts are committed every day in public schools, companies, and universities. And black people continue to serve six times the jail time for identical crimes as whites.

A patriotic country is a country that finds the flaws within itself and fixes them in order to strengthen the nation as a whole, and because these are the values we were supposedly founded upon. As it currently stands, America is not a patriotic country. It is a nationalist country, and the nation is white.

I'll salute the American flag and sing the national anthem when America truly salutes and embodies patriotism. There were black soldiers that served and fought for America in the war and came home and were lynched for wearing their uniforms. I'll salute and sing when America starts treating all people equally, without concern for race. I am all about helping make America more patriotic, but I call upon those born into white privilege to do the same. I'll salute and sing when America changes its ways and really lifts the stars and stripes.

"I'm only patriotic to the small piece of America that rolls with me."

—JERRY FORD

AFTERWORD

SOME FINAL THOUGHTS

This has been quite a journey. At the beginning of this book, I was a young kid on the streets of Detroit with nothing but my own determination to climb out of the ghetto and into the mainstream. With hard work, skills, drive, and bit of luck, I made something of myself. And now I am trying to reach back and help others do the same.

I now read or listen to two books per week. I have listened to all types of books, ranging from business how-to's to books on culture, finance, even the art of happiness. Some of them are bullshit and some are really dope. My message to you is, read/listen and then think for yourself, using my LAD technique (Listen, Analyze, and Decide). Take in the information, then decide for yourself if it makes sense.

This will help stretch your mind to another level, allowing you to continuously grow. Become the knowledge.

When I was writing this book, people kept telling me to watch my mouth and be careful what I say. Well, as you have witnessed, I didn't take their advice. No. I want all my readers to know exactly how I feel about things. Total honesty—never holding back—is the only way my message will be of use to anyone. I had something to say and I said it. Now it's your turn.

We human beings are creatures of emotion and not creatures of logic. We have our logical moments, but basically, it is our feelings that power us. They are what makes us human. It's important though, that when conducting business or making business decisions, you think with your head and not your heart. None of the advice I offer in this book is going to work for you if you let your emotions get the better of you—and that goes for the last chapter as well! We have to think hard and stay smart to change our lives and the world we live in. Your emotions provide you with your passion and drive; let them propel you forward so that your head can make you rich.

When you channel your energy toward something positive, people will feel the passion in whatever you do—whether it is a business venture, a book, or a piece of music. I personally channel my energy into writing and working out, as well as into my businesses. In the course of writing this book, I was conversing with another trainer and he expressed the belief that it isn't a good idea to work out while you're emotional—especially if you're upset. He said he thought that could be dangerous because you would be more prone to injury. I agree with him up to a point, but I also agree with Dale Carnegie, who said that we make use of only a small fraction of our bodies and minds at any given time. You can shape your emotions and channel that energy into your form, thereby preventing injury and getting stronger in the process. "I don't know where you're from," I told him, "but where I'm from it's life or death every damn day and you can't be at the mercy of your emotions."

When I pair the memory of that life-or-death world with Dale Carnegie's call to make better use of our bodies and minds, I end up with, "go HAM!" I look back at myself as a young boy—at all young boys—and say, "Young man, the human species is evolving. Look at our life expectancy. At one point it was no more than thirty or forty, and now...when somebody dies at seventy we shake our heads because he was so young. Bro, do you want to be a part of human evolution?! Do you want to continue to evolve—or do you want to stay where you are?"

Let's push for evolution.

People, your health and your wealth go hand in hand. "The proper physical exercise gives you a better chance at health and the proper mental exercise gives you a better chance at wealth," said Robert Kiyosaki in *Rich Dad, Poor Dad*. Remember, *health* and *wealth* are just one letter apart.

"Human evolution is like law—it changes every decade."

—JERRY FORD

ACKNOWLEDGMENTS

I would like to thank some of the people who helped make this book a reality, starting with my clients—especially the ones who provided me with positive feedback and "blurbs," and those who took the time to submit to an interview about their personal investment strategies. You inspire me. Thank you for allowing me to use your stories, words, and in some cases pictures. Deep thanks to Adrienne C. Moore for her generous contribution of an introduction, and to my editor, Laura Ross, for helping me communicate my ideas clearly and for her assistance in navigating the foreign country of book publishing. Special shout-out to Bill: Thank you for my bank account! Special props to my expert publishing company. Shout-outs to my parents, Mary Ford and Jerry Davis; and thanks to my brother, Shabazz Ford (aka Fatt Father), for always keeping me sharp. Finally, thank you, Joey Lee, Turron Kofi Alleyne, and Erin Kansy.

ABOUT THE AUTHOR

JERRY FORD grew up in the Detroit ghetto, where he earned a black belt in multiple martial-arts styles, winning gold medals in the Junior Olympics and other prestigious tournaments. A former top personal fitness trainer at the New York Health & Racquet Club and, later, for Equinox, Jerry has since launched his own private training business in Los Angeles, with a client list that includes celebrities, royal family members, and fighters across the globe. He is also a tremendously successful investor in stocks, real estate, television and film properties, and anything else he believes to be worth the risk.

Instagram: @RealJerryFord
Facebook: RealJerryFord
Twitter: @RealJerryFord